CHILDREN OF HEROIN ADDICTS

An Assessment of Health, Learning, Behavioral, and Adjustment Problems

Barbara J. Sowder
Marvin R. Burt

Praeger Studies in Issues and Research in Substance Abuse

General Editor:
James A. Inciardi

PRAEGER

PRAEGER SPECIAL STUDIES • PRAEGER SCIENTIFIC

Library of Congress Cataloging in Publication Data

Sowder, Barbara J
Children of heroin addicts.

(Praeger studies in issues and research in substance abuse)
Bibliography: p.
Includes index.
1. Children of drug addicts. I. Burt, Marvin R., joint author. II. Title. III. Series.
RJ507.N37S68 362.8'2 80-24408
ISBN 0-03-057033-6

Published in 1980 by Praeger Publishers
CBS Educational and Professional Publishing
A Division of CBS, Inc.
521 Fifth Avenue, New York, New York 10017 U.S.A.

0123456789 145 987654321

Printed in the United States of America

To the children and parents
who helped to make this study possible

PREFACE TO THE SERIES

During the decade of the 1960s, the use of drugs for the enhancement of pleasure and performance dramatically bounded from the more isolated corners of urban society to the very center of the traditional community. Drug taking and drug seeking became increasingly prevalent among numerous members of all classes and especially within the adolescent and young adult segments of the population. As the decade grew mature, the widespread use of drugs across the nation could no longer be left to speculation, and commentators of the era suggested that the phenomenon would persist and spread as a continuing fact of U.S. social life.

The logical causes of this rapid and encompassing swell in the use of drugs will never be fully understood, but what can be documented in this respect are the abrupt changes in the technology of drugs that served to usher in a new chemical age. These began in the early 1950s, and during the ensuing 15 years, an impressive array of newly compounded psychotropic agents were effectively introduced and enthusiastically promoted. The effect was to beset the consciousness of the U.S. public with a host of chemical temptations—sedatives, tranquilizers, stimulants, analgesics, hallucinogens, and synthetic narcotics—that could offer fresh inspiration and immediate relief from pain, anxiety, fatigue, sleeplessness, boredom, or tension. And concomitant with the arrival of this chemical age were new epidemics of heroin use throughout the urban and rural United States, which even further increased the awareness that ours was becoming an addicted society.

In direct response to the growing levels of substance abuse across the nation, federal efforts to cope with the problem reflected new initiatives in the areas of treatment, prevention, and research. Critical in this regard was the organization, during the early 1970s, of the National Institute on Drug Abuse (NIDA) in the Department of Health, Education, and Welfare, which was constructed to serve a major role in the support of treatment and research. Since that time, NIDA has been the primary funding source for research and treatment in the drug-abuse field.

In an effort to disseminate the results and findings of its strategies in treatment and research, NIDA has engaged in a broad publishing program, of which this series, Issues and Research in Substance Abuse, is a part. The series will be devoted to findings from NIDA-funded projects, and this work, Children of Heroin Addicts by Barbara J. Sowder and Marvin R. Burt, represents the inaugural volume. Additional volumes will be forthcoming, and comments and suggestions from our readers about this volume are welcome.

James A. Inciardi, Ph.D.
University of Delaware
Series Editor

PREFACE

This work on children of heroin addicts was funded by the National Institute on Drug Abuse (NIDA) under contract (271-76-4416) to Burt Associates, Incorporated. The study was initiated in August, 1976, and completed within a 12-month period. It involved children, parents, schools, and community agencies in five urbanized areas in the United States and represents the largest study yet undertaken on children of addicts.

It was, in many ways, a very difficult undertaking. The population of eligible addict parents proved to be smaller than anticipated, difficult to identify, and often fearful of participating in the study. Drawing a "matched" group of nonaddict parents and children from the same neighborhoods as addict families also proved more difficult than survey experts had anticipated. The field time for locating and interviewing the respondents was short (three months), and resources were limited. And, because so little research had been conducted on children of addicts or on addicted parents, there were few tried and tested measurements from which we could draw. We chose, therefore, to ask numerous questions of parents and children that would tell us something about the family environment, school adjustment, health, mental health, self-image, and various possible service needs of children of addicts and to compare the answers we obtained with the information gathered on the nonaddict group. Schools and various community agencies provided additional information on the study groups. The information collected on each parent/child represents over 1,200 variables.

Although this study is the largest body of information on children of addicts and their parents, we perceive it as only a beginning. There are many questions left to answer, and there are groups of addicts' children who have yet to be studied. The authors are currently engaged in another NIDA-funded study in these same urbanized areas to determine differences between children of addicts and nonaddicts in surrogate care (for example, foster care or informal relative care). Eventually, we will compare the subjects of this book with the subjects in our surrogate-care study.

It is our hope that the interest in children of addicts will not end with our endeavors and the types of studies described in the introductory section of this book. It is our firm belief, based on our studies of children of addicts, drug-abusing women, and family therapy with drug abusers, that addict parents and staff of drug treatment programs support the efforts to learn more about children of addicts and also strongly believe that the drug abuse treatment system needs to become more attuned to the service needs of these children and their families. It is our hope that the information contained in this book will help accomplish these ends.

Barbara J. Sowder, Ph.D., senior vice-president
Marvin R. Burt, D.P.A., president
Burt Associates, Incorporated
Bethesda, Maryland

ACKNOWLEDGMENTS

It would be impossible to adequately thank all of the individuals who assisted in this effort to learn more about the lives, problems, and service needs of children of heroin-dependent parents. The most direct contributions were made by the hundreds of parents and children who were the subjects of the study and by the staff of schools and community agencies who provided supplementary information on the children and their parents. We are especially grateful for the assistance in sample selection and for the information on heroin-dependent parents provided by the staff of eight drug treatment programs: Dayton BuDa and Project Cure, Dayton, Ohio; Desire Narcotics Rehabilitation Center, New Orleans, Louisiana; Metro East and its affiliate clinics, Harper and Riverside Drug Treatment Centers, Detroit, Michigan; Riverside General Hospital Drug Abuse Treatment Clinic, Houston, Texas; Project Reality, Salt Lake City, Utah; and Weber County Mental Health Center, Ogden, Utah. Similarly, we are grateful to the research divisions of the Boards of Education in Detroit, Houston, New Orleans, Salt Lake City, and Ogden for their assistance in our survey of schools attended by the children in the study.

Among those who made direct contributions were the staff of our subcontractors, Opinion Research Corporation (ORC), Princeton, New Jersey, and Applications Research Corporation (ARC), Dayton, Ohio. We are especially indebted to Stanley Zdep and Luci Agnese of ORC and Carolyn Szoke of ARC for taking a leading role in the interviewing and testing of children and/or parents.

Special thanks are extended to our consultants. Kuno Beller, M. Duncan Stanton, and Napoleon Turner provided invaluable assistance in questionnaire development. Meni Kolowsky, Fred Krause, and Lawrence Rubin contributed substantially by providing clinical ratings of the three-to-seven-year-old children's figure drawings. Rubin, in addition, reviewed the children's test-score sheets to assure that the tests had been administered properly by the examiners and provided clinical interpretations of the children's functioning, based on their tests.

We wish to acknowledge also the contributions made by the staff of the Services Research Branch, National Institute on Drug Abuse (NIDA). These extended beyond the funding that made this study possible. Their staff provided invaluable guidance and comments on the questionnaires and on reports submitted to them. We are especially grateful to Barry Brown, chief, and to Michele Basen, M.A., NIDA project officer.

Completion of this work would not have been possible without the devotion and hard work of Yukiko Carnes, Susan Dickey, and Elizabeth Hamilton of our staff.

The authors, and Burt Associates, Incorporated, are solely responsible for any errors of omission or commission in the reported findings.

We feel privileged to have been part of this worthwhile study. It has presented many difficulties and challenges—but also the promise of breaking "new ground" and of making a very substantial contribution to the field of drug abuse treatment.

CONTENTS

LIST OF TABLES

Table		Page

Table		Page

Table		Page

LIST OF FIGURES

INTRODUCTION

Our society has devoted a considerable amount of resources to the study, treatment, and legal curtailment of the heroin "addict." Much of what we have learned suggests that the unstable and impoverished lives of many addicts may place their children at risk for various developmental problems. Yet, when the authors reviewed the literature in 1976-77 it was apparent that few resources had been devoted to determining whether or not these children are a high-risk group.

Most research on children of addicts appears in the medical literature and pertains only to infants born to women dependent upon heroin or methadone during pregnancy. The findings suggest that this particular group of infants is indeed at risk. Compared to babies in the general population, these infants have higher rates of mortality, prematurity, low birthweight, congenital defects, and other health problems (Dickey in press).

These health problems may be caused, in part, by the lifestyles common among addicted women. Their high rates of prostitution lead to high rates of venereal diseases. These diseases increase their offsprings' chances of being spontaneously aborted, stillborn (even at term), or born with a congenital infection that may result in such disorders as deafness, scars, deformities, meningitis, arthritis, and infections of particular body organs. The tendency of addicted women to use unsterile needles when administering drugs also increases their infants' chances of developing hepatitis. In addition, these women are often malnourished, receive little, if any, prenatal care, and experience the many stresses associated with poverty and lack of social supports. These factors correlate substantially with high infant mortality and morbidity rates.

Like their mothers, these newborns may be addicted. During drug withdrawal, the infants are prone to feeding problems, restlessness, and irritability. They may be difficult to handle and provide little positive reinforcement when their mothers attempt to soothe them. Special care and patience, or even prolonged hospitalization, may be required to treat these infants. Because many addicted mothers lack the financial, social, and psychological supports needed to manage their infants, they may leave their babies in the care of relatives or relinquish them to foster care for varying periods of time (Dickey in press).

Whether or not the developmental risks found among neonates of addicted women affect their later development has been the subject of only six known follow-up studies (Ackerman 1976; Blinick, Jerez, and Wallace 1973; Lodge 1976; Strauss et al. 1976; Wilson, Desmond, and Verniaud 1973; Wilson, McCreary, Kean, and Baxter 1979). The sample sizes in these studies are small (generally less than 30 for any given test or variable); they tend to be based on different measurements; all are limited to preschool-aged children; and, except for the research by Geraldine Wilson and her colleagues (1979), all studies pertain to children born to women maintained on methadone during pregnancy. Because methadone treatment often brings women into prenatal clinics where they receive services that are not sought by or provided to many addicted women, it is possible that the follow-up findings on methadone groups are not representative of a large proportion of infants born to heroin-addicted women. It has been reported by Tovia Freedman and Loretta Finnegan (1976) that the provision of medical, nutritional, social, and psychological services to pregnant addicts seems to result in better developmental outcomes for their children.

Of the six follow-up studies cited previously, only two report physical problems among addicts' children. Wilson and her colleagues (1973) found unusually high rates of impaired somatic growth and equivocal neurological signs among a small group of children exposed to heroin in utero. Compared to several control groups, Wilson and her co-workers (1979) report that these children weighed less at follow-up, had smaller head circumferences, showed increased respiratory rates, and manifested more problems on a physical-adjustment scale. Milton Strauss and his colleagues found a difference in growth measures at age one between 21 children of methadone-maintained mothers and children of nonaddicted mothers. Although the group differences were not statistically significant, the methadone group was more likely to fall below the tenth percentile on height and weight. Children in the methadone group were also less likely to be walking by age one than were control children. Preliminary findings from cohort groups have shown similar growth lags in the methadone group. Blinick and his colleagues, however, found no physical problems among 14 four-year-old children of methadone-maintained women.

Wilson and her colleagues (1979) also report that 20 young children exposed to heroin in utero scored lower than controls on a perceptual battery. Ann Lodge cites similar findings from her longitudinal study of 45 children born to methadone-maintained women. These children also performed below average in fine motor skills. The methadone group studied by Strauss and his co-workers was found to score significantly lower than the control group on the Bayley Psychomotor Development Indices (PDI). There were also significant discrepancies between the methadone group's scores on the PDI and their scores on the Bayley Mental Development Indices, discrepancies that the controls' scores did not evidence.

All six follow-up studies show that addicts' children, as a group, scored average or above on IQ tests. Wilson and her co-workers (1979) do report that addicts' children scored lower than controls on some IQ measures but attributes this result to poor concentration and attention. Lodge also found that a poor attention span was common among her methadone group. She notes that language development was often above average in her sample, while Wilson et al. (1979) states that her group scored lower than controls on "organization skills" but not on the "receptive" or "expressive" subscales of the Illinois Test of Psycholinguistic Abilities.

Only Wilson and Lodge report on socioemotional adjustment. Wilson and her colleagues (1979) state that addicts' children exhibited more problems than controls on self- and social-adjustment scales. Lodge reports strong "oral" needs and immature play patterns among her sample but notes that these children were highly interested in people and objects. Lodge concludes that the children in her study have shown a "unique" pattern of development.

From these various studies, it appears that children of addicts may be at risk for developmental disorders. While the findings are not conclusive, research on the general population and on addict populations lends support to the assumption that children of addicts are a high-risk group.

When one considers the developmental problems prevalent among infants born to addicted women, it is apparent that some may be manifested at or before birth. For example, both venereal disease and hepatitis may be recorded as the cause of fetal and infant mortality and/or a number of birth defects in this group (Dickey in press). It has been noted previously that some of these problems are related to the life-styles of addicted mothers and, thus, may be preventable.

However, as indicated in research on the general population, many risk factors common to the lives of infants born to addicted mothers may take months or years to adversely affect development. It seems reasonable to assume that these risk factors are present also among some children of addicts who have not been exposed to heroin or methadone in utero.

One such risk factor is the early separation of the mother and infant, which seems to occur often after addicted women give birth. This interruption of the mother-infant bonding process has been shown to adversely affect the mother's child-rearing practices and the child's later cognitive development. The effects can be mitigated by special hospital programs that permit extended contact between the mother and infant (Klaus and Kennell 1976).

Whether or not the effects of early separation are mitigated when addicts' infants are placed in foster care is a question that remains unanswered. A high proportion of the children in the follow-up study of Wilson and her colleagues (1979) were in stable foster homes. Yet, they manifested some developmental problems and were prone to temper tantrums and disturbances of activity level, sleep, and attention span. Sol Nichtern (1973) reports similar behaviors among children of addicts placed in foster care at varying ages. Yet, David Fanshel (1975) found few problems among children of addicts placed at an early age in foster care. The only statistically signifi-can difference between these children and other groups of foster children was the greater likelihood of school adjustment problems in the addict group. One can conclude little about the effects of foster care on children of addicts from so few studies. However, from a review of literature on foster care in the general population, one can conclude that such placements often increase, rather than decrease, developmental risks among children (Kadushin 1974; Sowder 1977). Thus, placement in foster care may be another risk factor in the lives of children of addicts. The provision of comprehensive services to pregnant addicts and their families has been found to drastically increase the mother's ability to keep her infant and to provide the child adequate care. This was found to be the case for 80 percent of 300 women provided such services (Freedman and Finnegan 1976). Thus, the risks associated with foster-care placement also seem preventable for many children of addicts.

A major factor that adversely affects children's development is poverty. Children of addicts seem to face a high probability of growing up in poverty because of the low levels of education and job skills and the high rates of unemployment in the addict population (Burt, Glynn, and Sowder 1979; Chambers, Hinesley, and Moldestad 1970; Chein et al. 1964; Cuskey, Premkumar, and Sigel 1972; Ellingwood, Smith, and Vaillant 1966; Langrod 1970; Nurco and Lerner 1972; Vaillant 1970). Research shows substantial correlations between poverty and high postneonatal mortality rates (Sowder 1973), between poverty and high rates of marked or severe psychiatric disorders in children (Langner et al. 1974), and between poverty and malnutrition. Malnutrition lowers a child's resistance to disease, parasitic infections, and worms. It also increases emotionality and causes delays in cognitive and psychomotor development. Both malnutrition and poverty are associated with low educational attainment (Bee 1975; Scrimshaw 1968; Sowder 1973). Low birthweight and prematurity, common among poor children and addicts' children, are also additional factors associated with learning disabilities, lower IQ scores, and other health and emotional problems in older children (Sowder 1977).

Child abuse and child neglect are correlated with several of these risk factors, including prematurity, low birthweight, poverty, and mother-infant separation (Fanaroff, Kennell, and Klaus 1972; Klein and Stern 1971). Child abuse and neglect increase the risks of mortality and serious or permanent physical damage. Battered children may suffer emotional damage as well. They reportedly have difficulty establishing trust in others, are fearful (Martin 1972), gloomy, unhappy, immature, and prone to antisocial behaviors (Johnson and Morse 1974). A significant correlation has been found between abuse and neglect and delinquency (Burt and Balyeat 1976), and high rates of criminal behavior are noted among abusive and neglectful parents who themselves often have been abused as children (Gil 1974). Research on the general population shows that the delinquent and adult criminal behaviors of parents are positively correlated with delinquency among their children (Ahlstrom and Havinghurst 1971; California Youth Authority 1973; Glueck and Glueck 1950; Robins and Herjanic 1975).

There is, in summary, a tendency for different antisocial behaviors to be passed on from one generation to another. Such behaviors are commonly reported among addict populations. For example, addicts' lives are often marked by delinquency (Sowder 1977) and adult criminal behaviors (Burt, Glynn, and Sowder 1979). Many addicts report that they were physically abused or neglected as children (Sowder 1977), and exceedingly high rates (for example, 18 per 100 cases) of abuse among addicts' children have been reported from New York City (Beine 1974; Kaplan and Reich 1976), though much lower rates of abuse and neglect are reported for "drug-abusing" parents in national abuse/neglect demonstration programs (9 percent) and in cases representing a majority of the states (3 percent) (Cohn et al. n.d.).

Some researchers contend that the roots of addiction and deviancy lie in the addict's family of origin (Chein et al. 1964; Fagan et al. n.d.; Seldin 1972; Tennant, Detels, and Clark 1975) and that addicts tend to recreate the conflicted, deviant, and broken homes of their childhood when they marry (Chein et al. 1964; Clark et al. 1972; Cuskey, Premkumar, and Sigel 1972; O'Donnell 1969; Seldin 1972; Sullivan and Fleshman 1975-76; Taylor, Wilbur, and Osnos 1966; Vaillant 1966; Wolk and Diskind 1961). It seems likely that many addicts approach parenthood without having learned appropriate parenting skills from their parents and that this may introduce yet another risk factor into the lives of children of addicts. While addicted women appear eager to become mothers and are reluctant to relinquish their children for adoption (Eldred, Greer, and Berliner 1974; Fanshel 1975; Mondanaro 1976; Nichtern 1973), many are unable to assume proper responsibility for their children. It has been shown that these risk factors can be mitigated by the provision of parent education and comprehensive services to addicted mothers (Freedman and Finnegan 1976; Lief 1976). Unfortunately, few such programs exist. Those that are known affect mostly very young children.

The literature, in summary, told us very little about children of addicts. The research that had been conducted up to 1976 was focused largely on young children born to addicted women. There was little information about older children of addicts or about children who live with addicted parents but who were not necessarily exposed to heroin in utero. A study that includes these types of children was made possible by the National Institute on Drug Abuse and is the subject of subsequent chapters.

1
THE STUDY: PURPOSE AND METHODS

PURPOSE

This study was undertaken in 1977 to investigate two issues of interest to the National Institute of Drug Abuse (NIDA): whether or not three-to-seventeen-year-old children* of addicts are at greater risk than other children for health, learning, behavioral, socio-emotional, and/or adjustment problems and which types of intervention may be useful in preventing or treating any problems found among children of addicts and their families.

The study was the largest ever undertaken on children of addicts. It differed from most previous studies in that it was not limited to children exposed to heroin in utero, to those under age six, or to a sample in one city.

SAMPLING OF SITES, PROGRAMS, AND RESPONDENTS

Sites and Programs

In selecting sites, we sought the cooperation of drug abuse treatment programs that, first, were located in different geographical areas of the nation† and, second, treated a sufficiently large number

---

*The study was to include 18 year olds. However, since none appeared in the sample, the upper age limit was changed to 17.

†The criterion of geographical dispersion was chosen in order to obtain a better cross-representation of the population in terms of

of heroin-addicted clients from which a sample of 40 eligible parents per site could be obtained. Using these criteria, five urbanized areas were selected for this study: Dayton, Ohio; Detroit, Michigan; Houston, Texas; New Orleans, Louisiana; and Salt Lake City/Ogden, Utah.* (These sites are referred to hereafter by a number of protect the confidentiality of programs and clients.)

Respondents

The sources of information in this study were children, their parents, and the staffs of agencies and schools. The selection criteria and sampling of each respondent group are discussed below.

The Index Group

Sampling of the index group began with the parents. Eight large drug treatment programs in the five sites provided the parent sample pool.

The universe of eligible parent subjects in each program was composed of all clients with a history of heroin addiction who maintained parental responsibilities for at least one child aged three to seven (Site 1) or eight to 17 (Sites 2-5) who lived with them nine months or more during the year. Random sampling with substitution was used to select the parents. One child of each parent was chosen as the target subject. Where a parent had more than one eligible child, the target child was selected by random procedures. In addition, a subsample of three-to-seven-year-old siblings of the eight-to-seventeen-year-old target children was randomly selected for inclusion in the study. The sample sizes are summarized in Table 1.1. The procedures for screening for index-group eligibility and scheduling for interviews are detailed in Table A.1 of the Appendix.

About 20 percent of the clients contacted by the research team

---

sociocultural variables (for example, child-rearing practices) and to obtain some representation of persons of Hispanic origin.

*Originally, plans were made to include New York City as a sixth site. These plans were abandoned when the drug treatment program withdrew and a substitute program could not be located over a period of several months. This loss not only lowered the expected sample size but also greatly limited the interpretation of data on three-to-seven-year-old target children because it reduced the study of this group to one site.

TABLE 1.1

Parent/Child Sample

Site/Subject	Index	Comparison	Total
Site 1			
Target children (aged 3-7)	34	34	68
Parents	34	34	68
Sites 2-5			
Target children (aged 8-17)	126	126	252
Parents	126	126	252
Siblings (aged 3-7)	45	49	94
Total (all sites)	365	369	734

Note: Sample sizes varied by site. The number of families represented in each index and in each comparison group by site were 34 (Site 1), 17 (Site 2), 40 (Site 3), 29 (Site 4), and 40 (Site 5).

and/or drug treatment staff refused to participate in the study. The proportion of the refusals who actually fit the eligibility criteria for this study is unknown. However, drug treatment staff estimated that a sizable proportion of people they screened were ineligible because their children were not in their care. (The estimates varied by site from 10 to 50 percent of the parent clientele. It is not known how many of these children were with an "exspouse" and how many were with relatives or in foster care.) Of the refusals, 50 percent occurred in one site and about 25 percent at a second site. In each of these sites, the major reason for refusal was the clients' fear that their identities would not be kept confidential. The fear was founded on the fact that client confidentiality had been violated at these two sites by researchers in previous studies. The disclosure of the clients' addiction had led to loss of employment and/or rifts with family members among some clients. This experience, understandably, made many clients wary about participating in any research study. The few refusals at other sites seemed largely attributable to disinterest in the study and/or parents' concern about having their children tested or interviewed. The brief period (three months) available to locate and interview the sample did not allow time to work intensively with refusals to assure them that they would remain anonymous and not suffer any dire consequences by participating in the study.

The Comparison Group

The 160 comparison parents (see Table 1.1) were randomly selected from the immediate neighborhoods (within a radius of one to four blocks) where index families resided.* Inclusion in the comparison group was dependent upon several factors. One was the stipulation that there could be no history of drug abuse by either parent figure in a family since the time they assumed a parental role. This was determined by the self-report of a parent during the initial screening. Drug use of the actual parent respondent was again assessed by answers he or she gave to a battery of questions that were developed by the research team to distinguish addicts from nonaddicts. (Among the 160 parent respondents, only four [2.5 percent] answered this battery of questions as addicts answer them. This is less than the 5 percent who would be expected by chance to answer these questions as they would be answered by addicts.) This battery was tested with known addicts and nonaddicts in two sites before being used in the study.

In addition, the comparison group was matched to the index group by family structure (that is, one- as opposed to two-parent households) and, to the extent possible, age group of the target child. However, in Site 1, the sample pool was not large enough to match the three-to-seven-year-old groups precisely. In Sites 2-5, three age ranges were used in matching by age: eight to ten, 11 to 13, and 14 to 17. Moreover, an attempt to match comparison to index families by sex of the parent respondent was unsuccessful. It was often difficult to engage comparison fathers for an interview. Also, it was usually not possible to find a comparison match for single-parent index households in which the father was the only resident parent. (It was our original assumption that fathers would not be able to provide as much information about their children as mothers and that a bias would be introduced if groups did not contain equivalent proportions of mothers and fathers. Inspection of the data suggested that our original assumption was incorrect. "Don't know" responses were

---

*Selection of comparison samples from the same neighborhoods as "experimental" groups has been used successfully in other studies to assure equivalency between groups on such factors as ethnicity and income. As noted in subsequent chapters, this procedure failed to assure equivalency of income in this study.

rare and were no more likely to be given by fathers than by mothers.) The comparison children (see Table 1.1) were selected by the same procedures as the index children.

Most comparison parents were randomly selected from the Hanes Criss-Cross Directory and were initially contacted and screened for eligibility by telephone. (A total of 8,793 calls/contacts were required to locate the eligible comparison sample.) However, in two high-crime sites, it was necessary to supplement the telephone selection by sending interviewers with escorts into the neighborhoods, where they randomly screened and located qualifying respondents. The steps taken in sampling and scheduling comparison families for interviews are detailed in Table A.2 of the Appendix.

Approximately 11 percent of the eligible comparison parents selected for study refused to participate and/or did not show up for scheduled or rescheduled interviews. Reasons for the 11 percent refusal rate with the comparison parents are not totally known. However, a number of Site 1 contacts did express skepticism about the study. Some had kept appointments scheduled by a research team in a previous study only to find no one at the appointed place. They were wary of being misled again. The refusals at Site 1 accounted for almost 60 percent of the comparison-group refusals (and 25 percent of the index refusals). This refusal rate greatly affected our ability to match the three-to-seven-year-old groups by age. In two other sites, some of the refusals and/or broken contacts seemed to be attributable to the often expressed fear of crime in the neighborhood. Residents in these two sites reported that they were afraid to let strangers into their homes. In one site, it was necessary to abandon home interviews and rent the facilities of a neighborhood church for interviewing. Even here, church staff sometimes had to transport the participants, and/or we had to pay for the transportation of indigent participants. In the other high-crime site, drug treatment staff who were known to neighborhood residents were trained to interview in teams and/or assist our interviewers in order to facilitate admittance into respondents' homes.

Agencies and Schools

Agencies and schools were surveyed by mail. This involved three basically different types of questionnaires and, thus, different samples of respondents. One involved the staff of the drug treatment programs in which index parents were enrolled, another the schools that index and comparison children attended, and yet another the agencies that might be serving index and comparison children. The data presented on sample sizes for the drug treatment staff and the schools pertain to the number of index and/or comparison respondents rather than the number of treatment programs or schools.

TABLE 1.2

Response Rate on Drug Treatment Questionnaires

Respondent/Form/Questionnaire	Site 1	2	3	4	5	Total
Number of respondents	34	17	40	29	40	160
Number signing consent forms	19	15	34	29	27	124
Percentage signing consent forms	56	88	85	100	68	77
Number of questionnaires sent	19	15	34	29	27	124
Number returned	16	0	0	29	21	66
Percentage returned	84	0	0	100	78	53

Drug Treatment Staff. Table 1.2 shows the number and percentage of index parents who consented to our gathering information on them from drug-treatment staff and the number and percentage of questionnaires completed by staff on individual consenting clients. As shown, these questionnaires were not completed by all programs. The return rate represented slightly over half of the index parents, even though 77 percent consented to this survey.

TABLE 1.3

Percentage of Parents with Children in School Who Consented to School Survey: Sites 2-5 (in percentages)

Site	Index	Comparison
2	75	100
3	92	100
4	86	100
5	30	33
Total	70	79

Note: Figures are rounded and based on 120 index and 123 comparison respondents.

Schools. Table 1.3 shows the percentage of parents with children enrolled in school who consented to our survey of the schools in Sites 2-5. (Site 1 schools could not participate because teachers were involved in providing information for a lengthy court case.) As shown, comparison parents were more likely than index parents to consent to our sending a questionnaire to their child's school to gather information on the child (79 versus 70 percent). However, the differences between the groups on granting consent for the school survey were not statistically significant.

Table 1.4 shows the number of questionnaires mailed to schools and the number returned. (Because of the time constraints, the correct school districts for 13 questionnaires in Site 4 could not be identified before the closing of these schools. [There were many school districts at this site.] Thus, the number of questionnaires mailed out by the research team was 13 less than the number of consent forms obtained.) Of the 167 questionnaires mailed to schools, 104 (62 percent) were returned, and 95 (57 percent) of these contained usable

TABLE 1.4

Sampling Data on School Survey

Site	Number of Questionnaires Mailed		Response Rate (Percentage of Questionnaires Returned Completed)*	
	I	C	I	C
2	12	17	67	47
3	37	38	46	55
4	18	21	83	86
5	11	13	54	15
Total n	78	89	46	49

*Nine questionnaires not represented in the tabular figures were returned but were not completed. Only one represented a school's refusal to participate. This involved a comparison child. In five index and two comparison cases, the questionnaire could not be completed because the child, as named on the questionnaire, was not recorded as being in the school or the family had moved away. In another case, a Xerox copy had been made of a completed questionnaire and the ID number of the child was no longer distinguishable. This form was discarded by the research team.

tests used were the Bender-Gestalt, Peabody Vocabulary, Stanford-Binet Vocabulary Subtest, and the Draw-A-Person (Goodenough-Harris Drawing Test). They were selected for three reasons: they are widely accepted tests with established norms; they could be administered in a brief time period without overtaxing the short attention span of young children; and extensive data from these tests had already been collected in the sixth site scheduled for survey (but later abandoned), and these data were to form the sample pool from which a "matched" comparison group would be drawn at this site.

The Bender-Gestalt Test was used to assess perceptual-motor functioning. Skills required for good performance on this test are especially important in primary school, when children are learning the basics of writing and reading.

The Peabody Picture Vocabulary Test and the Stanford-Binet Vocabulary Subtest were used as two of the three measures of cognitive functioning. The former measures receptive language and provides an estimate of the child's verbal intelligence by measuring his or her hearing vocabulary. In contrast to the passive labeling required by the child on the Peabody, the Stanford-Binet Vocabulary Subtest provides an estimate of expressive language. It requires an action element in language organization; that is, the child must pay attention to his or her verbal product and match it to the adult's auditory model.*

The Draw-A-Person (DAP) Test was also used to assess cognitive functioning. It was chosen because it is less dependent upon vocabulary than the Peabody or Stanford-Binet and because it is considered by many clinicians to be more "culture free" than other tests for young children.† The figure drawings produced by children for

---

been a causal factor in the performance of children who scored poorly on the IQ and perceptual-motor tests.

*The Stanford-Binet Vocabulary Subtest is highly correlated (> .80) with overall intelligence quotient (IQ). The correlation between the vocabulary subtest and the total score on the Stanford-Binet Intelligence Scale is .65 for children at the sixth-grade level (Terman and Merrill 1973).

†The DAP and its predecessor (Draw-A-Man Test) have been used for many years. There are scores of reliability and validation studies on the different test versions. Validation studies have included children, adults, "normals," the retarded, psychiatric patients, and so forth. While correlations between the Draw-A-Man Test (which correlates substantially with the DAP) and other standard IQ tests used with young children are often substantial (> .60), some reported

this test also served as clinical measures of socioemotional/behavioral functioning. It should be noted, however, that their use as clinical types of measures is highly controversial and has not been well validated (Harris 1963).

The Eight-to-Seventeen-Year-Old Target Children

An interview schedule was devised for the eight-to-seventeen-year-old group to tap the youngsters' perceptions and opinions about themselves and others, their health, schooling, work, family interactions, friendships, drug and alcohol use, and so forth. Most items were developed specifically for this project. Some were modifications of items from other questionnaires. (These includes the Community Oriented Program Environment Scale (COPES), Group Atmosphere Scale and Family Atmosphere Scales developed by Rudolph Moos [available from Consulting Psychologists Press]; various instruments developed by researchers studying Head Start populations; clinical instruments sent to us by community mental health personnel; and the Jesness Inventory [available from Consulting Psychologists Press].) All items were pretested with appropriate respondents before field use.

The Sibling Group

A picture interview schedule—Robbie the Rabbit—was developed and pretested by the research team for use with the three-to-seven-year-old siblings of the eight-to-seventeen-year-old target children. An "introductory" picture of Robbie the Rabbit appears in Figure 1.1. The various Robbie pictures tapped the children's feelings about going to school, their family interactions, friendship patterns, trust in adults, and persistence at a task. In part, the questions were designed to determine whether the eight to seventeen year olds and their siblings perceived themselves and their families similarly or differently.

The Drug Treatment Staff

A questionnaire was developed specifically for this study to

---

correlations are substantially lower, perhaps because of differences in populations tested, score values, and so forth. Dale Harris, himself, states that important decisions about children (for example, placement in special education) should be based on one or more intelligence tests, not simply the DAP, which can supply additional information on severe intellectual and conceptual retardation (Harris 1963).

FIGURE 1.1

Introductory Picture of Robbie the Rabbit

obtain information from drug treatment staff on the services obtained by individual index parents and/or their families through the drug treatment programs and/or other community agencies. Items centered on types of treatment modalities in which index parents were enrolled within the drug treatment programs, length of treatment, goals of treatment, staff contacts and types of contacts with other family members, family counseling/therapy provided the index families by the program and/or other community agencies, and so forth. This was sent to staff only if the parent respondent consented. Copies of the questionnaire were shown to the respondents before asking them to sign a release form.

School Staff

The questionnaire for schools involved obtaining information on individual index and comparison children whose parents had signed a release form for obtaining this information. Many of the questions were taken from the school survey form developed by the Public Health Service (U.S. Department of Health, Education, and Welfare 1969). Other questions were designed specifically for this study by the research team. Questions focused on absences from school, achievement, classroom behavior, popularity with classmates, special services provided by the school and/or needed by the child, and so forth. Accompanying materials to schools stated that this was a study of children's needs being conducted for the U.S. Department of Health, Education, and Welfare (HEW). No mention was made of NIDA or of the drug abuse of parents.

Forms for Other Agencies

The types of forms sent to other community agencies were outlined in Table 1.5. These were intended as "validation" forms. Each form focused on "validating" the parents' responses to specific questions appropriate for the types of agencies listed in Table 1.5. These questions for parents were:

> During 1976, did this child receive mental health services from a mental health center, mental hospital, psychiatric ward, or child guidance clinic in the area?
> During 1976, was this child's name recorded by the court, police, or a social service agency as being a victim of child abuse or neglect?
> During 1976, was this child brought into court because of delinquent behavior?
> During 1976, was this child on probation?
> During 1976, did this child receive drug treatment services?
> During 1976, did this child receive alcohol treatment services?

Similar questions were inserted into the letters to appropriate agencies, together with a general description of the purpose of the study. The description stated that this was a study of children's needs for HEW. No mention was made of NIDA or the drug abuse of parents. With the forms on mental health, abuse/neglect, and delinquency, we generally sent the names of all index and comparison children. (A few parents in two sites did not give any names. Also, in Site 1, we could send out only five index names since, in keeping with the question of an "addict committee," consent had to be obtained from parents to send names to these agencies and only five parents consented.) Only names of children aged 14 and above were sent with the forms for drug and alcohol treatment. Names were listed in Group 1 and Group 2 categories. Respondents were not told what these numbers represented. Respondents were informed that one or two "false" names were interspersed among real names on the lists to help ensure confidentiality. (The "false" names were actually composite names of persons known to the research staff. They were uncommon names but no more so than many of the real names of the children under survey. The "false" last names used did not appear in the telephone directory in the site for which they were chosen.) The agencies were requested to report only the number of children in each group whose names appeared in the 1976 case loads of the agencies.

Field Procedures

Parents and Children

Two interviewers were assigned to each parent/child group or, in the case of Site 1, one clinician and one interviewer per family. One interviewer focused on the parent, the other on the child or children. Interviews with the parents took 30 to 45 minutes and were held in a room separate from the child. Interviews with eight-to-seventeen-year-old children usually took approximately 30 to 40 minutes; the Robbie the Rabbit schedule, eight to 12 minutes; and the administration of the test battery, 45 minutes to one hour.

The interviews for the index group were held in a central location (usually the drug treatment center but, in some cases, a neighborhood church). Interviews with the comparison group in two sites (1 and 3) were also held in a central facility (that is, a church). In other sites, interviews were held in the homes of comparison parents. Parent respondents, their eight-to-seventeen-year-old children, and three-to-seven-year-old children administered the test battery were given $10 each for participating. The young children responding to the Robbie the Rabbit questionnaire were paid $5. Parents and children were told that all answers provided by the children to the interviewers would be kept confidential and not revealed to the parent or anyone outside the research team. However, upon request, Site 1 parents could obtain information on their child's test results and a list of agencies that would treat any problem indicated by testing. They were informed also that it was a screening test, not a final diagnosis of any problem, and that screening tests sometimes provide invalid data. Moreover, parents were told that everything they said would be kept confidential.

In screening the three-to-seven-year-old children with the test battery, care was taken on the part of the clinicians to ensure that test results were an accurate reflection of achievement capacity rather than a measure of the duration of attention span (this required considerable care with index children). Several traditional techniques were employed to overcome a child's short attention span. Before testing, parents were given instructions to see that the child had a good sleep the night before the test and that the child was adequately fed before the test. If the child seemed restless or overactive, the child was permitted to move about the room and explore the environment before testing began. An introductory conversation was generally used to establish rapport and relax the child so the child could devote maximum attention to the test. At appropriate periods, the child was allowed to "stretch." This permitted a natural break in concentration and helped the child return to the task refreshed. Encouragement was given throughout the test with judicious reinforcement of the child's efforts (not simply successes). However, "bribery" was not used since offering a reward for a child's cooperation has been shown to introduce a contaminating factor into testing data. (Parents, of course, may have offered their child all or part of the $10 payment to gain participation. This factor could not be controlled but should be considered.) In three cases, the examiner could not establish rapport with the child. Another examiner was then called to complete the testing. The other examiner was successful in two cases. The third child was totally uncooperative. This child was excluded from the study, and a substitute was selected.

The testing of three-to-seven-year-old children was not done blindly; that is, the examiners were aware of the fact that they were testing children of addicts. The index children were tested in a drug treatment program. This was in keeping with the parents' desires and the desires of an "addict committee" whose members wanted all procedures to be clearly known to participating clients. Blind testing, in summary, was not possible. However, the tests administered required no clinical interpretation (except for the interpretation of the figure drawings, which was done blindly by three clinicians who were not known to the test examiners). The Bender-Gestalt and three IQ tests' scores were thoroughly reviewed independently by a highly experienced clinician who was not involved in the testing. This clinician found the test scores to be complete, accurately scored, and unbiased.

Drug Treatment Staff

The questionnaires for the drug treatment staff were mailed to the programs during the ninth month of the 12-month study. Programs in Sites 4 and 5 responded quickly. Others were hard pressed by staff demands to meet the time deadlines and, as noted in Table 1.2, could not respond in the time frame allotted.

School Questionnaires

The survey for schools could be initiated only two to three weeks before schools closed. In Sites 2, 3, and 4, questionnaires were distributed by the research divisions of the boards of education but were mailed directly back to the research team by individual schools. In the other site, questionnaires were mailed directly by us to individual schools.

Community Validation Forms

Community validation forms were mailed at the same time as the school forms (that is, once all children's names were available). A follow-up letter was sent one month later.

In using all the above forms, confidentiality was assured to all respondents—parents, children, and agencies.

DATA ANALYSIS

There were three general types of data to be analyzed: interview data, clinical data, and mail survey data.

Interview Data

Initially, frequency distributions were run on each variable included in each interview instrument. The frequency distributions were then inspected to determine appropriate categories and cross-tabulations. Cross-tabulations were then conducted on each variable. The data were then analyzed and placed in table format as appropriate.

Statistical tests of significance were conducted (chi-square and t tests) as appropriate. The significance level of .05 was chosen as the threshold for statistical significance. Where expected cell frequencies were too small for statistical testing using chi-square, no additional tests (for example, Fisher's z) were conducted because of time and cost constraints. Therefore, in subsequent chapters, it will be stated that no statistical tests were performed on some variables because of small cell sizes.

Factor analyses were conducted using selected variables. A variable was selected on the basis of there being a hypothesized relationship between it and at least one other variable and/or on the basis that the analysis had shown that index and comparison groups were (statistically) significantly different on that variable. The factor analysis was conducted using the Verimax rotation. In addition, discriminant analysis was used in analyzing the data on Site 1 children and their parents to determine what variable best distinguished the index and comparison groups. Covariance analysis was also used with Site 1 data.

Clinical Data

Several types of assessments were made of the test scores and figure drawings of three to seven year olds in Site 1.

Separate Test Analysis

The scoring systems used for the Draw-A-Person IQ and Peabody Vocabulary Tests are based on established norms. The scores and accompanying classificatory systems appear in Table A.4 of the Appendix. Each child's score was recorded on each test. The t test was used to determine whether differences between groups on the Draw-A-Person IQ and Peabody Vocabulary Tests were statistically significant.

The Stanford-Binet Vocabulary Test was scored using the child's "mental age" (MA), that is, the age range into which her or his score fell according to established norms. Three categories of rating a child were used: above average (the test score was above the norm for the chronological age or CA), average (the MA was within the norm for the CA), and below average (the MA was below the CA). The t test was used to determine whether differences were statistically significant between index and comparison groups using the three categories above and to determine whether differences between CA and MA within each group were statistically significant. Because of the small sample sizes, "below average" was considered to be "below the tenth percentile."

The scoring system for the Bender-Gestalt perceptual-motor test is highly dependent upon age. The age norms (that is, average number of errors) used in this study are shown in Table A.5 of the

Appendix.* Because so few index children scored above average on this test, only two scoring categories were used in the statistical testing of these data. These were "average and above" and "below average." Each child's score was based on the scoring system used. (A mean score was not used because the number of age groups within the small samples would have yielded subsamples too small to permit statistical testing.) The chi-square test was used to determine differences between the index and comparison children who scored "average and above" and those who scored "below average."

Analysis of Performance across Tests

Because the results from one test on very young children are often invalid and unreliable, the most meaningful "screening" technique is to examine children's performance on a battery of tests, such as those used in this study.† Therefore, each child's performance across the four tests was examined. Children were then classified into one of four "categories," using test scores as a basis for this classification. The classifications and criteria upon which they were based are "high risk," children who fell below the tenth percentile for their age on three out of four tests or all four tests; "moderate risk," children who did not fit the high-risk category but did not score average or above on at least two out of four tests; "average-low average," children who scored somewhere in the average range on two or more of the tests (scoring average on only two tests defined "low average"); and "superior-bright," children who scored above average on three or four tests.

Descriptive statistics were used to present the findings using these four categories. Because of low cell frequencies, the four categories were collapsed into two for purposes of statistical testing: "at risk" (high risk and moderate risk) and "average-superior." The chi-square test was used to investigate the magnitude of the differences between the index and comparison children within these two groups.

---

*The age norms used were established on a large, low-income multiethnic population and are far more "liberal" than the generally used Koppitz norms. For example, the scoring for a six year old using norms shown in Table A.5 allows almost twice as many errors as the Koppitz norms (compare Koppitz 1971).

†Errors still occur using a "screening" battery. Children who appear to be at risk because of poor performance on several tests should be further tested by various types of professionals to verify screening results.

Several separate analyses were performed on the index children considered "at risk" using selected variables (see Chapter 2). The "at risk" group was then compared to the "average-superior" group using the chi-square test, where cell sizes permitted the use of inferential techniques.

Clinical Assessment

Blind assessments were made by three clinicians of the socio-emotional status of each child as judged by the child's figure drawings on the Draw-A-Person Test. All were highly qualified and experienced clinicians.

In assessing the figure drawings, each judge was asked to consider the following attributes in assigning each child's drawings to one of four categories: the size of the figure, pressure of the line, placement on the page, theme, exactness, degree of completion, detailing, symmetry, midline emphasis, perspective, proportions, shading, line reinforcement, erasures and content (which consisted of all the individual parts of the body, as well as the facial expression and postural tone of the figure), and age level of the child and developmental expectancy for the given age level.

Using these criteria and their clinical experience, the judges assigned each child to one of four categories: no behavioral and developmental problems, mild behavioral and developmental problems, moderate behavioral and developmental problems, and severe behavioral and developmental problems.

The research staff's criterion for classifying the children was that at least two of the three clinicians assign the same score to an individual child. In only one case did all three raters totally disagree. In all but four cases of disagreement, only a one-point difference was made in the rating. (On the "severe problem" category, agreement was especially high. Of the index children in this category, 82 percent were so judged by <u>all</u> three raters. The corresponding figure for comparison-group ratings was 75 percent.) The overall interrater reliability figures are shown in Table 1.6.

After the clinicians' ratings for each child were categorized, the chi-square test was used to determine whether or not there were statistically significant differences between index and comparison children.

Clinical and testing data were also subjected to discriminant analysis, together with some data gathered through parental interview. This was done for 28 cases in each group for which complete data existed on all variables chosen from parent interview schedules.

TABLE 1.6

Interrater Reliability on Figure Drawings

Rater	Index	Comparison
Rater 1 versus rater 2	.84	.79
Rater 1 versus rater 3	.81	.86
Rater 2 versus rater 3	.80	.70

Mail Survey Data

Drug Treatment Staff Questionnaire

Because of the low response rate obtained through the questionnaire of the drug treatment staff, only descriptive statistics (for example, frequencies, percentages, and averages) were used to analyze these data.

School Questionnaire

The chi-square test was used, where appropriate, to determine whether there were statistically significant differences between index and comparison children in school performance, absenteeism, and other variables reported upon by teachers. In instances where cell frequencies were too small to permit statistical testing, descriptive statistics were used (for example, frequencies and averages).

Community Validation Forms

Simple frequency counts were used to assess the community validation forms. Because the possibility existed that the same child could be in the case load of more than one agency for a particular type of treatment (for example, abuse and/or neglect), the range of responses is presented in subsequent chapters (that is, the lowest and highest number obtained from the combined agencies in one site that treat a particular problem).

LIMITATIONS OF THE STUDY

Any survey is beset with problems and limitations that affect the interpretation of results and the extent to which one can generalize from study populations to the "universe" of persons that the selected samples supposedly represent. This survey is no exception. Field time was limited as were resources. Resulting limitations were small sample sizes at some sites, exclusion of children under age three, exclusion of rural areas, nonrepresentation of some ethnic groups, the fact that not all self-report data could be validated, and so forth. These and other problems and limitations, as well as "solutions" or steps taken to minimize them, are summarized in Table A.6 of the Appendix.

2
THE THREE-TO-SEVEN-YEAR-OLD CHILDREN AND THEIR FAMILIES: SITE 1

What can be learned about the young children of heroin addicts and their families through the use of developmental screening tests, their parents' self-reports, and selected information from community agencies? In what ways, if any, will these children and families differ from matched comparison children and families randomly selected from the same neighborhoods?

These were the basic questions underlying the survey in Site 1. Because Site 1 represents the only focus on the developmental screening of young children, the results are presented separately for this group in this chapter. The findings are based on very small samples from only one city in the United States. The small sample sizes and other methodological limitations discussed in Chapter 1 greatly hinder drawing firm conclusions from these data. Nevertheless, as will be indicated throughout this chapter, many of the findings are consistent not only within Site 1 but with the findings reported for eight to seventeen year olds and their families in Sites 2-5 (see Chapter 3). The discussion begins with an overview of the demographic and other characteristics of the Site 1 parents and their "spouses" (that is, married and unmarried partners).

BACKGROUND AND CHARACTERISTICS OF PARENTS

Table 2.1 summarizes the information on the sex, age, racial/ethnic origin, marital status, educational level, employment, and income status of the 34 index and 34 comparison parent respondents and/or their spouses.

The 34 index parent respondents were evenly divided by sex, whereas 71 percent of their comparison counterparts were female.

TABLE 2.1

Selected Characteristics of Site 1 Parent Respondents and Spouses (in percentages)

Characteristic	Group Index	Group Comparison
Sex[a]		
Male	50	29
Female	50	71
Age[a]		
18–25	26	26
26–30	38	26
31–35	21	12
36–40	6	24
41–45	6	12
> 45	3	0
Race/ethnicity[a]		
Black	15	23
White (non-Hispanic)	82	68
Other	3	9
Marital status[b]		
Married	35	67
Living with someone	38	18
Living alone	26	15
Respondent's years of education[a]		
< 9	5	3
9–12	74	71
> 12	21	27
Spouse's years of education[a]		
< 9	4	3
9–12	60	52
> 12	28	45
Don't know/refused	8	0

(continued)

Moreover, fewer index than comparison parents were age 35 or older (21 versus 38 percent). These differences were not statistically significant. These same trends were found across Sites 2–5, where statistically significant differences occurred between groups on these variables.

TABLE 2.1 (continued)

Characteristic	Group Index	Comparison
Respondent's employment[c]		
Employed	24	53
Not employed	76	47
Spouse's employment[a]		
Employed	52	66
Not employed	48	34
Family income (1976)[d]		
< $5,000	47	15
$5,000-$7,999	23	23
$8,000-$13,999	21	30
> $13,999	0	23
Don't know/refused	9	9

[a]Not statistically significant.
[b]$\chi^2 = 7.1$, df = 1, p = .03.
[c]$\chi^2 = 6.2$, df = 1, p = .01.
[d]$\chi^2 = 10.6$, df = 2, p < .01.

Note: Figures are rounded, and calculations for each major category are based on 34 index and 34 comparison respondents or 25 index and 29 comparison spouses/partners.

More Site 1 index than comparison parents were black (82 versus 68 percent). However, racial/ethnic differences were not statistically significant here or in any of the sites surveyed.

Index parent respondents differed significantly (p = .03) in marital status from comparison respondents (as they did across Sites 2-5). Site 1 comparison parents were twice as likely as index parents to be married, while index parents were slightly more than twice as likely to be "living with someone." There were no significant differences between groups in terms of single- versus two-parent households, as expected, since this was a matching criterion for selecting comparison families.

Most respondents and their spouses had completed between nine and 12 years of schooling. However, more comparison than index parents had over 12 years of education (27 versus 21 percent). Similarly, more comparison than index spouses had more than 12 years of schooling (45 versus 28 percent). These differences in educational levels were not statistically significant. Similar trends were noted across Sites 2-5 with regard to the educational levels of index parent respondents and their spouses.

Unemployment was high among these families. However, index respondents were significantly ($p = .01$) more likely to be unemployed than comparison respondents (76 versus 47 percent). Index spouses were also more likely to be unemployed than comparison spouses (48 versus 34 percent), but this difference was not statistically significant. These trends held across Sites 2-5, where, contrary to Site 1, it was the index spouses (rather than the respondents) who were significantly more likely to be unemployed.

Almost 50 percent of these 34 index families lived on an income of $5,000 or less in 1976. Only 15 percent of the comparison families were this poor. Altogether, 70 percent of the index families lived on less than $7,999 in 1976, compared to 38 percent of the comparison families. No index families had incomes above $13,999, whereas 23 percent of the comparison families had incomes above this level. The income differences were statistically significant ($p < .01$), as they were also across Sites 2-5. The reported figures represent 1976 income before taxes for all family members from such sources as work, public assistance, and unemployment insurance.

The index and comparison parents and spouses also differed substantially in terms of their arrest histories *since* assuming a parental role. (The data exclude traffic violations.) Except for two "don't know" responses among comparison respondents, answers from this group indicated that neither the parent respondents nor their spouses had any arrest histories. The picture was quite different

TABLE 2.2

Arrest History of Site 1 Index Parent Respondents and Spouses

Arrest Status	Respondent	Spouse
Ever arrested since becoming a parent	68%	31%
Drug-related arrest	(35%)	(16%)
Nondrug-related arrest	(35%)	(20%)
Refused to answer	(0)	(4%)
Mean number arrests per arrestee	1.65	3.12

Note: Figures are rounded and based on 34 respondents and 25 spouses.

for the index group (see Table 2.2). Over two-thirds of the respondents and 31 percent of their spouses had been arrested since assuming a parental role. Slightly over one-third of the index respondents had been arrested for drug-related offenses and about one-third for nondrug-related offenses. The figures reported for spouses were lower; 16 percent had drug-related arrests and 20 percent had nondrug-related arrests.

As expected from the study design, there was no evidence of drug use among the comparison respondents or their spouses since they had assumed a parental role. Table 2.3 depicts drug use among the index group. As shown, 44 percent of the index target children reportedly were exposed to drugs in utero, 29 percent were exposed to heroin either singly or in combination with other drugs, and 18 percent were exposed only to heroin. Of the mothers who used heroin, 60 percent did so for six to nine months during pregnancy, and one-third used heroin throughout their pregnancy. Among seven out of ten women who used heroin less than eight months, five used it in the first trimester, three in the second trimester, and two during the third trimester.

Index respondents varied as to the age at which they began using heroin. The mean age of initial use was 20.7. Since becoming a parent, 32 percent of the respondents said they had had trouble with drugs other than heroin (barbiturates, cocaine, marijuana, methadone, tranquilizers, amphetamines, and "others"). Of the index spouse group, 24 percent reportedly had had trouble with drugs since assuming a parental role, and all but one of these had received treatment for the drug problem.

In summary, index parents were more likely to have had fewer years of schooling, to be of minority group status, and to be living below the poverty level than comparison parents. These factors alone have been correlated with increased "risk" for children in such areas as educational achievement, health status, and psychological functioning (Sowder 1977). Added to these risk factors are others: the rather high rates of arrest among the index respondents and their spouses, a high rate of maternal drug use during pregnancy with the target children, and the current drug problems of the respondents and some of their spouses.

The differences between index and comparison respondents in terms of certain demographic variables (family income, parents' employment, parents' years of school) raise questions about the extent to which the groups are comparable. The results of multiple discriminant analyses and covariance analysis (reported later in this chapter) indicate that these variables do not (with some exceptions) explain very many of the differences between the two groups. Further, differences in these variables among index children judged to be at

TABLE 2.3

Drug Use History of Site 1 Index Parent Respondents and Spouses (percentages)

Drug Use Variable	Percentage
Drug use of mother during pregnancy with target child (n = 34)[a]	
Any drug	44
Heroin only	18
Other drugs only[b]	15
Heroin and other drugs	12
Age respondent began heroin use (n = 34)	
15–17	21
18–20	32
21–24	26
25–30	21
Respondent with other drug problems since becoming a parent (n = 34)	32
Spouse with drug problems since becoming a parent (n = 25)	24
Spouse receiving treatment for drug problems since becoming a parent (n = 6)	83

[a]Categories are not mutually exclusive.

[b]Includes use of such drugs as marijuana, barbiturates, amphetamines, cocaine, and "other drugs" several times a week "for at least one month" during the pregnancy.

Note: Figures are rounded.

risk versus those who are not were not statistically significant, as indicated later in this chapter. The problem of comparability of index and comparison groups is discussed further in Chapter 3.

FAMILY STRUCTURE

It has already been noted that the index households were less likely than comparison households to have had a spouse living in them (26 versus 15 percent) but significantly more likely to have had an unmarried partner living in them (38 versus 18 percent). (Nine [26.5 percent] of the index parent respondents reported living in a drug treatment center at the time of the interview. It is suspected that some shifting alliances occurred between the time of screening for eligibility and the time of interview since the application of matching procedures after screening for eligibility should have assured greater equivalency between index and comparison groups on the one- versus two-parent household variable.) Of the index and comparison respondents, 36 percent and 26 percent, respectively, had been living with their spouses and/or partners less than nine months. Index households were less likely than comparison households to have had no adult other than the parent respondent living in them (26 versus 15 percent). Differences between groups on these variables were not statistically significant.

Comparison households were more likely than index households to contain grandparents of the child and other relatives (32 versus 21 percent), but this difference was not statistically significant. The average length of stay for grandparents and other relatives in both household groups was quite long—a range of eight to 17 years—suggesting that some parent respondents had had relatives living with them for most or all of their "married" lives. Data presented later suggest there may have been more reliance on extended family members in the index group in terms of child rearing. This trend occurred also across Sites 2-5.

In summary, these data suggest that there may have been more family instability in the index group than in the comparison group. Index parents were less likely to be married and more likely to be living alone or with an unmarried partner, and more members of this group had been living with their spouse or partner less than nine months at the time of interview. These trends are consistent with those found across Sites 2-5.

Site 1 index parents had an average of approximately 2.5 children under the age of 19. The corresponding figure for comparison parents was 2.9. The difference may be partly attributable to the fact that more comparison parents were age 35 and above. (Across Sites 2-5, each group had an average of approximately one additional child compared to these Site 1 groups.) Only 5 percent of the Site 1 index children and 1 percent of the comparison children were not living with the parent respondent. These few children were living with another parent or relative. The same percentage of children in each group was also living away from the parent respondents' home across Sites 2-5. Most were with other parents or relatives.

The 34 index children tended to be younger than their comparison peers. Compared to 27 percent of the comparison group, 55 percent of the index group were between the ages of three and four. Among the comparison group, 73 percent were between the ages of five and seven, as compared to 45 percent of the index group. Also, more index children were girls (62 versus 44 percent). The sex difference between the index and comparison children was not statistically significant, nor were age differences when one compared groups within each age year (that is, three, four, five, six, and seven). However, more index children fell into the younger group ($\chi^2 = 4.9$, df = 1, $p < .05$).

According to parent respondents, only three (9 percent) of the index and four (12 percent) of the comparison target children were not the respondents' children by birth.

CHILD-REARING PRACTICES AND PARENTAL EXPECTATIONS

Parents were asked a number of questions about the rearing of the three-to-seven-year-old target children and/or other children in their family, their expectations and hopes for their children, their disciplinary practices, and the people or agencies involved in helping them raise or support the children. Some questions were specific to the target child, simply because it was too time-consuming to ask parents about their child-rearing practices and/or expectations for each child. Other questions, where applicable, were generalizable to more than one child.

Parents in both groups were often in agreement as to the age at which their child should be able to accomplish certain tasks (see Table 2.4). Two-thirds or more of the parents in both groups stated a child should be age 13 or older before working part-time or before taking care of younger siblings when parents were away from home. Of the parents in each group, 75 percent or more stated a child should be age 16 or older before being allowed to decide how late to stay out at night or before taking a full-time job. Comparison parents were significantly ($p = .009$) more likely than index respondents to state that a child should begin helping around the house by age two (68 versus 26 percent), while more index than comparison parents chose ages three to five as appropriate for this task (50 versus 20 percent). Of the index and comparison parents, 15 percent and 6 percent, respectively, did state that a child could stay alone in the house under age 12. This would be considered lack of supervision (child neglect) by some state laws and some professionals. A sizable proportion of index and comparison parents reportedly expected their child to be able to feed himself or herself before the age of two (49 versus 76 percent), and 41 percent in each group expected the child to be toilet trained before the age of two. The findings are generally consistent with those reported across Sites 2-5.

The majority of parents in both groups reportedly had high hopes for their children in terms of education, marriage, parenthood,

TABLE 2.4

Expectations of Child on Different Tasks by Age: Site 1
(percentages of parents responding)

	Age of Child																			
	< 1		1		2		3–6		7–10		11–12		13–15		> 16		Don't Know		Total	
Task	I	C	I	C	I	C	I	C	I	C	I	C	I	C	I	C	I	C	I	C
Feed him/herself	20	20	29	56	32	20	18	3	0	0	0	0	0	0	0	0	0	0	99	99
Be toilet trained	6	9	35	32	44	59	15	0	0	0	0	0	0	0	0	0	0	0	100	100
Help around the house*	6	3	9	9	26	68	50	20	9	0	0	0	0	0	0	0	0	0	100	100
Have a part-time job	0	0	3	0	0	0	0	0	6	3	9	15	18	41	62	38	3	3	101	100
Have a full-time job	0	0	3	0	0	0	0	0	0	0	0	0	0	0	76	82	20	18	98	100
Stay alone in the house	0	0	0	0	3	0	0	0	12	6	24	38	18	32	35	20	9	3	101	99
Decide how late he/she can stay out at night	0	0	0	0	0	0	0	0	3	3	0	3	6	3	76	76	15	15	100	100
Take care of younger children when parents are away	0	0	0	0	0	0	0	0	3	6	20	18	26	35	41	35	9	6	99	100

*$\chi^2 = 13.6$, df = 4, p = .009.
Note: Figures are rounded and in each row are based on n = 34 in each group.

TABLE 2.5

Parental Hopes and Expectations for Child: Site 1
(in percentages)

Thing Child Might Do in Future	Index		Comparison	
	Like	Expect	Like	Expect
Finish high school	68[a]	65[b]	97[a]	8[b]
Go to college	88	59[c]	88	16[c]
Get vocational training	18[d]	9	56[d]	28
Get married	47[e]	47[f]	82[e]	16[f]
Be a good parent	59[g]	38[h]	91[g]	12[h]
Make a lot of money	59	23	65	20
Have a career of military service	18	9[i]	15	40[i]
Have a career in sports	29	12[j]	41	48[j]
Have a "helping" career	47[k]	15	71[k]	16
Have a career[l]	3	0	18	2

[a] $\chi^2 = 10.119$, df = 1, p = .001.
[b] $\chi^2 = 19.198$, df = 1, p = .0001.
[c] $\chi^2 = 10.949$, df = 1, p = .0009.
[d] $\chi^2 = 10.690$, df = 1, p = .001.
[e] $\chi^2 = 9.273$, df = 1, p = .002.
[f] $\chi^2 = 6.202$, df = 1, p = .01.
[g] $\chi^2 = 9.490$, df = 1, p = .002.
[h] $\chi^2 = 5.017$, df = 1, p = .03.
[i] $\chi^2 = 8.151$, df = 1, p = .004.
[j] $\chi^2 = 9.571$, df = 1, p = .002.
[k] $\chi^2 = 3.886$, df = 1, p = .05.
[l] Response to an "other" category.

Note: Figures are rounded and based on n = 34 in each group.

TABLE 2.6

Use and Extent of Different Disciplinary Practices by Site 1 Parents (in percentages)

Type of Discipline	Daily		3–4 Times a Week		Once in a While		Never		Total	
	I	C	I	C	I	C	I	C	I	C
Send to room or set in chair	12	18	15	18	44	38	29	26	100	100
Slap or hit with hand	9	9	9	3	50	44	32	44	100	100
Talk to or lecture	65	41	9	21	26	38	0	0	100	100
Yell at	41	26	9	15	38	50	12	9	100	100
Take away privilege (e.g., television)	0	0	12	6	53	50	35	44	100	100
Whip with belt, switch, object	3	3	9	9	53	44	35	44	100	100
Threaten with whipping*	53	21	18	12	21	50	9	18	101	101

*$\chi^2 = 10.4$, df = 3, p = .02.

<u>Note</u>: Figures are rounded. Calculations in each row are based on n = 34 in each group.

financial success, and so forth (see Table 2.5). A sizable proportion of the index parents expected their children to accomplish these things. Few comparison parents expressed high expectations for their children. There were, in fact, a large number of statistically significant differences between these groups in terms of what they would like their children to do and their expectations of the children. Comparison parents were significantly more likely than index parents to report that they would like their child to finish high school ($p = .001$), have vocational training ($p = .001$), get married ($p = .002$), be a good parent ($p = .002$), and have a "helping" career in which they can serve other people ($p = .05$). However, they were significantly less likely than index parents to expect their child to do any of these things, except to have a career in the military and in sports ($p = .002$). Parent groups did not differ in terms of their desire for their children to obtain a college education. However, index parents were significantly ($p = .0009$) more likely to say they expected their children to get a college education.

In summary, as a group, comparison parents appeared considerably more ambitious for their children than index parents, but they were far less likely to say they expected their children to accomplish their wishes. While the index parents had higher expectations of their children than comparison parents, their expectations were lower than their desires for their children on all items except "get married." These desires and expectations of Site 1 parents differed in many ways from those reported by parents across Sites 2-5. Why this was so cannot be determined from the available data.

Index and comparison parents in Site 1 did not differ greatly from one another in their reported methods of disciplining children (see Table 2.6). The majority relied most frequently on oral methods (for example, lectures, "yelling" at the child). In this respect, index parents were significantly ($p = .02$) more likely than comparison parents to threaten their child with a "whipping." However, use of physical punishment was reportedly relied on "only once in a while" or was "never" used by over 80 percent of the parents in both groups. Similarly, the majority of the parents reported only infrequent use of such punishments as denying the child something (for example, watching television) or isolating the child (for example, sending the child to his room). These findings are consistent with those reported across Sites 2-5.

As shown in Table 2.7, index parents were less likely than comparison parents to have rules about what the child should eat (62 versus 73 percent). This difference between groups was not statistically significant, but it was a trend not found across Sites 2-5. The most common punishment for disobeying rules about eating was to

TABLE 2.7

Punishments for Disobeying Rules about Eating
as Reported by Site 1 Parents
(percentages responding "yes")

Type of Punishment	Index	Comparison
Child is denied a wanted food (e.g., dessert)	43	68
Spank/whip	9	8
Nothing	5	12
Make child sit until food is finished*	14	0
Take away something child wants (e.g., going out)*	9	12
Give lecture on why food must be eaten*	19	0
Total	99	100

*Response to an "other" category in the questionnaire.

Note: Figures are rounded and based on 21 index and 25 comparison respondents.

deny some food the child liked (for example, dessert). This was also true across Sites 2-5.

In Site 1, index parents were more likely than comparison parents to rate themselves as either "very strict" (15 versus 3 percent) or "not strict at all" (15 versus 6 percent) in their child-rearing practices. The differences were not statistically significant. Across Sites 2-5, index parents were more likely to rate themselves as "a little strict" or "not strict at all."

Index parents in Site 1 also were more likely than comparison parents to say they did not raise their children the way their parents raised them or did so "only a little" (39 versus 21 percent). Differences between groups were not statistically significant. This same trend appeared across Sites 2-5, where the differences between groups were statistically significant.

The majority of index and comparison parents in Site 1 reportedly spent 12 hours or more a week with their child (59 versus 62 percent). These differences between groups were not statistically significant. The similar differences found across Sites 2-5 were statistically significant. As noted below, this phenomenon may be related to drug use.

In about 75 percent of all Site 1 households, the spouse/partner was helping to raise the target child at the time of interview (see Table 2.8). However, grandparents were more likely to be involved in the rearing of index than comparison children (62 versus 41 percent), as were "other" relatives (23 versus 15 percent). These group differences were not statistically significant. These same trends appeared across Sites 2-5. However, in the latter case, index grandparents and "other" relatives were significantly more likely than their comparison counterparts to be helping to raise the children.

As can also be noted in Table 2.8, index parents were significantly ($p = .004$) more likely than comparison parents to be receiving financial support for the target child from welfare agencies (65 versus 29 percent). Grandparents and "other" relatives were also more likely to be providing financial assistance in the index families, but these group differences were not statistically significant. These same

TABLE 2.8

Types of People Helping to Raise and Financially Support the Three-to-Seven-Year-Old Children (in percentages)

Type of Person/Agency	Index	Comparison
Helping to raise child		
Spouse/partner	73	76
Child's grandparents	62	41
Other relatives	23	15
Child's older sibling	15	18
Friends/neighbors/others	9	9
None of the above	9	3
Providing financial support		
Male household head	50	65
Female household head	38	53
Child's grandparents	35	18
Other relatives	12	3
Welfare/public assistance	65[a]	29[a]
Child's father[b]	0	6

[a] $\chi^2 = 8.5$, df - 1, $p = .004$.

[b] Response to an "other" category. Presumably these cases represent broken homes.

trends appeared across Sites 2-5 where index families were significantly more likely to be receiving financial support for the children from grandparents as well as welfare agencies.

Two-thirds of the index respondents reported that their drug use had kept them from being the kind of parent they would like to be. Among these 22 parents, drug use had prevented 68 percent of them from providing a "better financial situation" for their children, 45 percent also stated that their drug use kept them from being able to "spend enough time with their children" or "provide them proper care," and 18 percent said it had made them "emotionally unfit" to be the kind of parent they would like to be. Similar reports were obtained across Sites 2-5.

PARENTS' PERCEPTIONS OF CHILDREN'S FRIENDS AND ACTIVITIES WITH FRIENDS

Parents were asked about the friendship patterns of the target children, including the number of the child's friends they had met, visiting patterns of these friends, and whether or not the parents disapproved of some of the child's friends.

The parents' reports suggested that all but 9 percent of the index and 3 percent of the comparison children had one or more friends and that the parents had met most of these friends. However, 29 percent of the index target children reportedly "played alone" most of the time. "Playing alone" was not reported for this comparison group or for any of the children across Sites 2-5.

There was a slight tendency for comparison children's friends to visit their home more frequently than for the index children's friends to visit them. Of the comparison and index children's friends, 82 percent and 76 percent, respectively, visited their homes at least once a week. Slightly over 90 percent of these children played games or cards with their visiting friends. Comparison children were significantly more likely to engage in sports with their friends than were the index children ($\chi^2 = 5.8$, df = 1, p = .02). This finding may be related to the fact that comparison children tended to be older. Across Sites 2-5, it was the index group that was more likely to engage in sports when friends visited their homes.

Few parents disapproved of the target children's friends. Comparison parents were more likely than index parents to say they did not disapprove of "any" of their child's friends (85 versus 56 percent). However, 35 percent of the index parents said they disapproved of "almost none" of their child's friends, as did 12 percent of the comparison parents. These types of differences were not statistically significant, as they proved to be across Sites 2-5.

ASSESSMENT OF CHILDREN'S COGNITIVE, PERCEPTUAL-MOTOR, AND SOCIOEMOTIONAL STATUS AS JUDGED BY TEST PERFORMANCE

The measures of the children's performance on four tests provided a rich source of information on the children's cognitive, perceptual-motor, and socioemotional functioning. The picture that emerges is often in stark contrast to the parents' portrayal of these children.

Cognitive development was measured in this battery of tests by the Draw-A-Person IQ Test, the Peabody Picture Vocabulary Test, and the Stanford-Binet Vocabulary Subtest. Perceptual-motor skills were measured by the Bender-Gestalt Test. Appropriate age norms were used to judge each child's performance on each of these tests. Clinical assessments of each child's social and emotional functioning were made blindly by three clinicians largely on the basis of figure drawings on the Draw-A-Person Test (see Chapter 1 for discussion).

The testing results generally represent 33 index and 34 comparison children. One index child was omitted from the comparative analyses of test scores because of a recording error. On the test forms, this boy's age was recorded as six years and three months. On the parent interview schedule, the figures were reversed (that is, three years and six months). If this child were in the six-year age range, he would fall within the "high-risk" group discussed later in this chapter. If he were in the three-year age range, he would be classified in the "high-average" group on three tests (though he would still have performed poorly on the Bender-Gestalt). There is reason to believe this child is yet another child at risk because of the qualitative assessment of his performance on various tests. A clinical profile of this child (number 0237) appears in Figure 2.1. Hereafter, he is excluded from the discussion of the testing results.

Comparisons of Index and Comparison Children

Cognitive Status

As a group, the index children didn't perform as well as the comparison children on tests measuring cognitive abilities.

Table 2.9 shows the mean scores of the index and comparison children on the Draw-A-Person IQ and the Peabody Vocabulary Tests. The Draw-A-Person mean for the comparison group was within the "average" range (90-109), while the mean for the index group was in the "low-average" range (75-89). As the t test shows, the difference between groups was statistically significant ($p < .0005$). On the Peabody test, the comparison group tended to fall into the "average

FIGURE 2.1

Clinical Profile of Child Number 0237

Responses to the Peabody

1. An "envelope" is "something you wear in the rain."

2. A "puddle" is "where you go when they hit you."

Figure Drawings

The figure drawings were hollow, unhappy-looking people. The nose and mouth were not drawn on two of the figures. Arms were drawn of unusual length and were attached to the body at the waist. Hands and feet were not drawn. The figures convey feelings of helplessness and lack of stability, feelings of emptiness and great unhappiness.

Bender-Gestalt

The Bender-Gestalt was replete with perserverations (the same circles drawn over and over again for different geometric designs), and there were problems with angulation. The child was unable to use space efficiently by drawing all the designs on one page.

Source: The profile was supplied by Lawrence Rubin, Maimonides Community Mental Health Center.

learner" category (90-109), whereas the index group tended to score in the "slow learner" category (75-89). However, differences between groups on the Peabody were not statistically significant.

Table 2.10 shows the percentages of each group who scored below average and above average for their age on the Stanford-Binet Vocabulary Subtest. Close to two-thirds of the index children scored below average for their age compared to approximately one-third of the comparison group. Further, 59 percent of the comparison children scored above average for their age compared to only 15 percent of the index children. The t test differences were statistically significant ($p = .0009$). To further analyze these data, within-group comparisons were made on the children's chronological age (CA) versus

TABLE 2.9

Mean Scores of Site 1 Children on the Draw-A-Person and Peabody Vocabulary Tests

Test	Group Mean Score		t	df	p
	Index	Comparison			
Draw-A-Person	77.2	90.9	4.556	65	< .0005
Peabody Vocabulary	86.7	94.5	2.941	65	NS*

*Not statistically significant.

Note: Each test score is based on a total n of 33 index and 34 comparison children.

their mental age (MA) as judged by their test scores. As shown in Table 2.11, the mean MA (3.4) of the index children was below their CA (4.5). The difference was statistically significant ($p < .01$). The comparison group, on the other hand, had a mean MA (6.2) above its CA (5.3). This difference, too, was statistically significant

TABLE 2.10

Performance of Site 1 Children on the Stanford-Binet Vocabulary Test (in percentages)

IQ Range	Index*	Comparison*
Below average	61	32
Average	24	9
Above average	15	59
Total	100	100

*$t = -3.47$, $df = 65$, $p = .0009$.

Note: Figures are rounded and based on 33 index and 34 comparison children.

TABLE 2.13

Socioemotional Ratings of Site 1 Children
Based on Figure Drawings
(in percentages)

Problem Category (Rating)	Index	Comparison
No problem (1)	19	42
Mild problem (2)	6	27
Moderate problem (3)	39	18
Severe problem (4)	35	12

Notes: Figures are rounded and based on 31 index and 33 comparison children. Three sets of figure drawings were lost in the mail, hence the smaller sample size as compared with other tabular presentations. When categories 1-2 versus 3-4 are used, differences between groups are statistically significant ($\chi^2 = 12.3$, df = 1, p = < .001).

for their age on this test (p = .01). In fact, 24 (73 percent) of the index children fell below the tenth percentile for their age on this test as compared to 12 (35 percent) of their comparison peers. These findings suggest that many children, particularly in the index group, may experience difficulty in such school tasks as writing.

Socioemotional Status

The following discussion represents a clinical assessment of the Draw-A-Person figure drawings of the three-to-seven-year-old target children. It is based on the blind ratings of three clinical psychologists and the criteria discussed in Chapter 1. The controversies surrounding the clinical use of the Draw-A-Person Test are also discussed in Chapter 1 and will not be repeated here.

As shown in Table 2.13, the clinical ratings suggest a poorer socioemotional prognosis for the index children than for the comparison children. Because of the small sample sizes, the "no problem" and "mild problem" categories were combined as were the "moderate problem" and "severe problem" categories in order to perform a chi-square test. Results of this analysis showed that the index group

FIGURE 2.2

Figure Drawings of Mother by Comparison Children

Figure a
Child aged seven
years, two months

Figure b
Child aged five
years, two months

Figurc c
Child aged six
years, one month

was significantly more likely than the comparison group to be rated in the "moderate-severe problem" category ($p < .001$). Interrated reliability was high, as shown by the reliability coefficients presented in Chapter 1.

A more detailed study of the figure drawings was done by Lawrence Rubin of Maimonides Community Mental Health Center. The discussion that follows mainly reflects Rubin's clinical judgment. He noted that the figure drawings of the comparison group were more "vigorous and alive" than those of most index children. The tone of their figures was generally pleasing, as shown in Figure 2.2. Many productions of the index children were far below the Goodenough-Harris age norms. Figure drawings of the index children were often rigid, tense, asymmetrical, and constricted. Conflict and anxiety were expressed in the large number of erasures, the random and, at times, feverish shading, and the aggressive reinforcement of lines.

Many of the three- and four-year-old index children merely made some scratches on the paper or scribbled in an uncontrollable manner over the sheet. Figure 2.3 shows two such drawings of boys in the "high-risk" index group discussed later in this chapter. Some of the older index children drew stick figures where only the head was differentiated. Figure 2.4 shows two such drawings of index children who scored average or average and above on two out of four tests. In some of these stick drawings, the figures are without arms, the bodies are hollow, and there is little differentiation of body parts or clothing.

The facial features of the index children's drawings were for the most part rigid, constricted, and immobile. Many of the bodies were fragmented, schematized, or broken, with oddly shaped heads. Figures often had unhappy faces. Many of the productions were disfigured and grotesque, with gross distortions of the ears, hands, arms, and/or feet. The hands, used to master the physical environment, were in many cases long and weak. According to clinical criteria, this suggests a tremendous need for support from the environment but no active manipulation of it. Several children almost "glued" the arms very close to the body. This suggests guilt, insecurity, and fear reactions. Some drew fingers as claws (suggesting aggression) or as petallike and unmanipulative. Other index children presented circles for hands that are unmanipulative and unfunctional. (Additional examples of the index group's drawings appear in Figure 2.5.)

In Rubin's judgment, the data pointed also to isolation, anger, and loneliness among many children in the index group. Their approach to the test battery tasks, figure drawings, and verbalizations suggested that they viewed themselves as worthless, untrustworthy, and unable to do even the smallest things properly. They appeared to feel insecure in most social situations (perhaps because of mistrust and poor social judgment). They seemed to show little zest in learning

FIGURE 2.3

Figure Drawings by Three-Year-Old, High-Risk Index Children

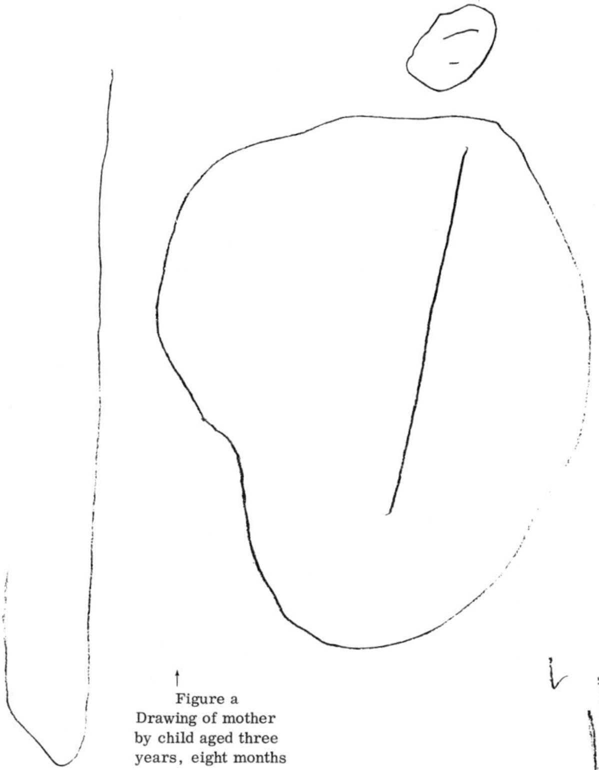

↑
Figure a
Drawing of mother
by child aged three
years, eight months

Figure b →
Drawing of father
by child aged three
years, eight months

FIGURE 2.4

Representative "Stick" Figure Drawings by Index Children

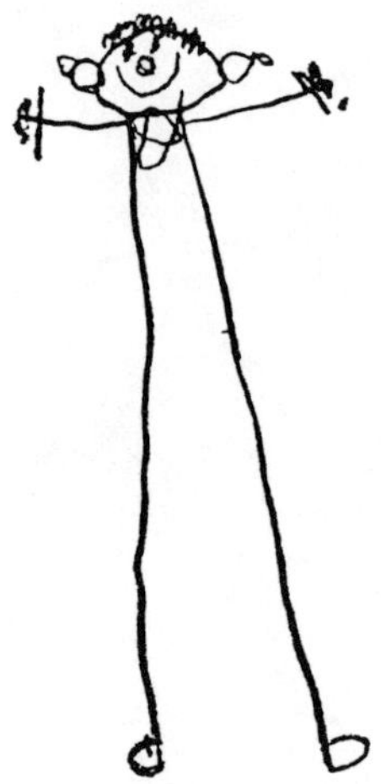

Figure b
Drawing of mother
by child aged five
years, three months

Figure a
Drawing of self
by child aged seven
years, six months

FIGURE 2.5

Additional Examples of Figure Drawings by Index Children

Figure a
Drawing of a man by "high-risk" child aged six years, one month

Figure b
Drawing of self by "above average" child aged five years, five months

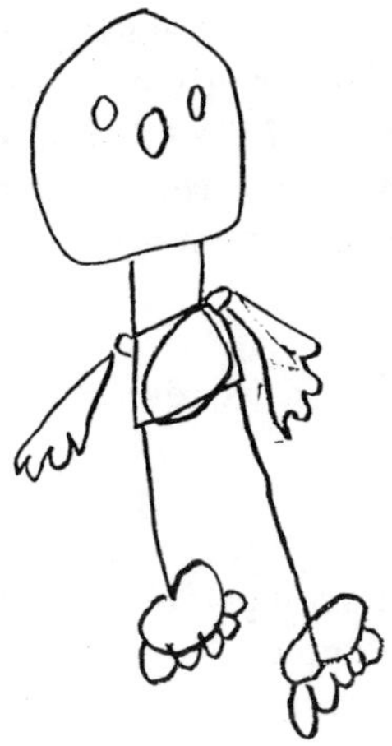

Figure c
Drawing of mother by "average" child aged seven years, eleven months

Figure e
Drawing of mother by "high-risk" child aged five years, nine months

Figure d
Drawing of self by "above average" child aged five years, seven months

new skills or mastering reality and appeared unable to perceive themselves and the world correctly. For some, the world seemed to be perceived as a dangerous and unhappy place in which to live.

In addition to the above social factors suggested by the clinical assessment, it should be noted that the index children presented a different clinical impression than the comparison children to the two examiners who tested the children. The index children were less well-groomed, it was difficult to establish rapport with them, they had difficulty relating to adults, and, most importantly, they had noticeably shorter attention spans. Far more time and care were required on the part of the examiner to try to assure that the test results were an accurate reflection of the achievement capacity of these children rather than a reflection of the duration of their attention span.

"Risk Scores" among Target Children

Testing of very young children is difficult (see Chapter 1). Therefore, one must be wary of the results from any one test. Much more meaningful and valid, we believe, are scores for each child on a number of tests. The authors, with the assistance of Lawrence Rubin, carefully examined the individual performance of each index and each comparison child on all the three IQ tests and the Bender-Gestalt Test to determine children who may be classified in some "risk" category. Two "risk" categories were determined: "high risk" and "moderate risk." The former means an individual child fell below the tenth percentile on at least three out of the four IQ tests. "Moderate risk" means a child did not fall into the "high-risk" category but did score below the "average" level on at least two tests (see Chapter 1).

Table 2.14 shows some gross classifications of the index and comparison children based on their individual performance on each of the four tests (that is, their performance level across tests). Because of low cell frequencies, statistical testing could be performed using only two categories: "high risk" and "moderate risk" versus "average-low average" and "superior-bright." Using these categories, a chi-square test showed that the comparison children performed significantly better than did the index children ($\chi^2 = 5$, df = 1, $p < .02$).

These particular data strongly suggest that 14 index children (42 percent of the group) suffered from neurologic deficits, mental retardation, and severe emotional problems. They were, essentially, at "high risk." Another five (15 percent) of these children were at "moderate risk." While screening can only alert us to children at risk, the data suggest that this group of 19 index children fall into a

TABLE 2.14

Site 1 Children in Different Risk Categories
Based on Scores across Tests
(in percentages)

	Index	Comparison
High risk[a]	42	20
Moderate risk[b]	15	9
Average-low average[c]	33	35
Superior-bright[d]	9	36

[a]Fell below tenth percentile on at least three out of four tests. Eight of these 14 children fell below the tenth percentile on all four tests.

[b]Did not fit the high-risk category but did score below average on at least two of the four tests.

[c]Scored within average range or above on at least two tests.

[d]Scored superior-above average on at least three out of four tests (most scored above average on four tests).

"risk" group whose prognosis for early school success and socio-emotional development is indeed poor.

The Index Risk Group

An effort was made to discover possible causal factors for poor test performance within the index group. The index children were divided into two groups, "at risk" (n = 19) and "superior-average" (n = 14) based on their combined performance on the Bender-Gestalt and the three IQ tests (see above). Data were inspected to search for variables that might possibly differentiate these two groups and/or were shown in previous studies to be related to cognitive or perceptual-motor deficits in children. These variables are listed in Table 2.15. Where cell frequencies permitted, the chi-square test was used to determine if there were statistically significant differences between the two index groups. As indicated in the table, only one statistically

TABLE 2.15

Relationships between "Risk" Status and Other Study Variables within the Site 1 Index Group (in percentages)

Study Variable	Risk Group	Average-Superior Group
Child's age[a]		
< 6	16	50
> 6	84	50
Child's birthweight[b]		
< 6 Pounds	32	7
> 6 Pounds	58	86
Don't know	10	7
Child plays alone most of time		
Alone	42	14
Not alone	58	86
Child is in school		
In school	26	44
Not in school	74	56
Race/ethnicity		
Black	84	79
Other	16	21
Mother used heroin during pregnancy		
Used	32	21
Not used	68	79
Mother used other drugs during pregnancy[b]		
Used	42	7
Not used	58	79
Don't know	0	14
Mother used heroin and/or other drugs during pregnancy		
Used	47	29
Not used	53	71
Family income in 1976		
< $5,000	58	36
> $5,000	37	57
Don't know	5	7

(continued)

TABLE 2.15 (continued)

Study Variable	Risk Group	Average-Superior Group
Parent respondent and/or spouse employed		
Employed	47	64
Not employed	53	36
Parent respondent and/or spouse arrested since becoming parent		
Arrested	63	71
Not arrested	32	29
Don't know	5	0
Spouse/partner helps raise and/or support child		
Helps	74	71
Doesn't help	26	29
Parental financial support for child		
Neither parent	53	21
One or both parents	47	79
Grandparents and/or other relatives help raise and/or support child		
Helps	74	71
Doesn't help	26	29

[a] $\chi^2 = 4.5$, df = 1, $p < .05$.

[b] Low cell frequencies prohibited statistical testing of group differences.

Note: Figures are rounded. Calculations for each variable are based on 19 "risk" children and 14 "average-superior" children (as judged by test performance).

significant difference was found; that is, index children at risk were significantly ($p < .05$) more likely to be below age six than those of the "superior-average" group.

The results of these statistical tests should be viewed with considerable caution, of course, because of the small sample sizes. The age factor, however, may be an important one, partly because of its possible relationship to "cognitive deprivation." It can be noted from a reading of the table that the risk children were less likely than their peers to be in school. An inspection of the data shows that only one of the children judged to be at "high risk" (that is, fell below the tenth percentile on three or all four tests) was in school. The other four "risk" children in school were classified as "moderate risk." Also, of the ten children who "played alone" most of the time, eight were in the "risk" group, and, of these, five were in the "high-risk" group. It is possible that these "risk" children, especially the "high-risk" children, were more isolated than other children, that there was less "cognitive stimulation" in their homes, and that entrance into and/or continuation in school will modify their risk status. This, of course, is only conjecture but appears to be a hypothesis worth testing with larger samples in future studies.

It is also possible that some of the differences between the group at risk and the "average-superior" group would have been statistically significant if they had occurred in a larger population. It can be noted that the "risk" group was more likely than the "average-superior" group to have weighed less than six pounds at birth, to have been subjected to drugs in utero, to be living in a family whose income was below $5,000 in 1976, to have parents who were unemployed, and to be in a family where neither parent provided financial support for the child. Inspection of data not shown in Table 2.15 did not indicate that there was more abuse in the "risk" group than in the "average-superior" group. Only one of the three reported abuse cases occurred in the "risk" group. Similarly, only one of the four neglect cases appeared in the "risk" group. Nor were the children at risk overrepresented among those index children who visited emergency wards in 1976.

In summary, the available data did not shed much insight into why a large proportion of the index children were considered to be at risk on the basis of their test performance. The "cognitive deprivation" hypothesis appears worth further exploration. It might be added, in this context, that the first statement made by Rubin when he examined the test data was, in essence, that many children in this group appeared never to have experienced a high level of verbal exchange with adults. This remark preceded his reading or knowledge of the other findings reported by the authors.

SCHOOL AND PRESCHOOL STATUS OF TARGET CHILDREN

Only 44 percent of the index target children were in school at the time of interview compared to 62 percent of their comparison peers. The difference between groups was not statistically significant and is probably attributable to the age differences between the groups.

Most of the youngsters in school were in kindergarten or first grade (87 percent of the index and 95 percent of the comparison children). Approximately 75 percent of these comparison children and 87 percent of the index children had missed some school because of illness during the school year. A significantly higher proportion of comparison than index children had missed six or more days of school for some unspecified reason (86 versus 7 percent; $\chi^2 = 22.9$, df = 4, $p = .0001$). More index than comparison children reportedly had missed school because they "skipped or didn't want to go" (13 versus 5 percent) or because they were "told not to come by school staff" (7 versus 5 percent). These two differences could not be tested statistically because of small cell sizes, but it is worth noting that the same trends were found across Sites 2-5.

A majority of the parents whose children were in school thought their child was doing "very well" in most school subjects. This rating was given by 53 percent of the index parents and 62 percent of the comparison parents. All remaining parents rated their child as doing "fair" in most school subjects. The differences between groups were not statistically significant. A similar trend was found across Sites 2-5.

Two school honors had been awarded to the Site 1 index group compared to 11 honors awarded to the comparison group. This difference cannot be accounted for totally by the difference in enrollment between the groups. This disparity between groups in winning awards or honors was not noted across Sites 2-5. (One index child and three comparison children were honor students. The index child had won a spelling award. All other honors or awards were represented in the comparison group and consisted of general "good performance" awards [n = 3], attendance awards [n = 2], a leadership award [n = 1], awards in a specific subject [n = 1], and "other" [n = 1]. It is possible that the same child may be represented in more than one category. This was not tested for specifically because of time and cost constraints.)

All comparison parents and 87 percent of the index parents whose target children were in school said they had personally visited their child's school. Although most parents had not been contacted by the schools, there were more contacts among the index group for such things as misbehavior or absences. For example, three index parents and one comparison parent had been contacted because of their child's "misbehavior in school," and two index parents (and no comparison parents) had been contacted because their child was absent or "skipped" school. Small cell frequencies prohibited statistical testing of these data. These data on school staffs' contacts with parents follow the trend reported across Sites 2-5, where similar differences between the index and comparison groups were usually statistically significant.

Several of the index and comparison children were receiving such services from the schools as counseling (7 versus 9 percent), special education (13 versus 9 percent), individual help with school subjects (20 versus 19 percent), and special programs to help them catch up (13 versus 5 percent). Group differences on these variables were either not statistically significant or could not be tested because of small cell sizes. However, it is worth noting that a higher proportion of the index group was receiving each of these services except counseling. Across Sites 2-5, index children were more likely than comparison children to be receiving counseling and individual help with school subjects, but they were less likely to be receiving special education and programs to help them catch up, despite the fact that they appeared to have more school-related problems than did comparison children. The reasons for these differences by site cannot be determined from the information gathered.

Of the Site 1 index children and comparison children, 15 percent and 12 percent, respectively, were enrolled in a preschool program at the time of interview. According to parents in both groups, all but one comparison child liked preschool "a lot." These children especially liked "learning things and games" and "being with other children." Index children were more likely than comparison children to be receiving special services from the preschools (for example, special classes, counseling, medical services, and free meals). In fact, eight services were provided to this index group while only one service was provided to a comparison child.

In Site 1, 41 percent of the index and 26 percent of the comparison children were neither in school nor preschool. The parents of these index children were more likely than their comparison counterparts to say that their child was not in preschool because the child was too young (64 versus 33 percent). About 80 percent of these children generally spent their weekdays at home playing with toys (78 versus 21 percent) and watching television (55 versus 29 percent). Small cell frequencies prohibited statistical testing of these data.

PHYSICAL HEALTH STATUS OF TARGET CHILDREN AND UTILIZATION OF MEDICAL SERVICES

Several questions were asked the parent respondents regarding the health of the target children and their utilization of medical services. These included questions about birthweight, premature birth, problems at birth that required medical attention, current health status, and visits to medical facilities and medical practitioners.

According to parents' reports, 21 percent of the index and 9 percent of the comparison children weighed less than six pounds at birth. Small cell sizes prohibited statistical testing on this variable. Although the data are not precisely comparable, this low birthweight figure for the index group is exceptionally high when compared to the percentage of live births in the low birthweight* range among the general population in 1975 (7.4 percent) or among the black population in 1975 (13.1 percent) (U.S. Department of Health, Education, and Welfare 1975). This figure is also higher than the figure reported across Sites 2-5 for index children (19 percent) or comparison children (18 percent) who weighed less than six pounds at birth.

A much larger proportion of index than comparison children also required medical services at birth (29 versus 9 percent). This figure for the index group considerably exceeded corresponding figures across Sites 2-5 (13 percent for each eight-to-seventeen-year-old group). Five (15 percent) of the Site 1 index children were reportedly drug addicted at birth, a figure somewhat comparable to that reported for index children addicted at birth (12 percent) across Sites 2-5.

Index parents were significantly more likely than comparison parents to rate their child's present health as only "fair" or "good" (62 versus 35 percent) rather than "excellent" ($\chi^2 = 7.2$, df = 2, p = .03). This is a partially different trend from that found across Sites 2-5, where index parents were significantly more likely than comparison parents to rate their child's health as either "excellent" or as "fair-poor." The types of current health problems among Site 1 index children were mostly those of vision, hearing, emotional, and "other." Table 2.16 shows the data on vision and hearing problems reported by parents. These data suggest a higher incidence of vision and hearing problems among the index group. These problems, of course, may have adversely affected the test performance of these children. This possibility was not considered in the analyses of the data because

*Low birthweight is officially defined as five pounds and eight ounces (U.S. Department of Health, Education, and Welfare 1975). "Less than six pounds" was used in this survey to simplify the interview.

TABLE 2.16

Eye and Ear Problems among Site 1 Children (in percentages)

Problem*	Index	Comparison
Eyes		
Wears glasses/contact lenses	9	9
Need glasses	12	0
Had eye infections/ other problems	9	3
Ears		
Slight hearing problem	6	3
Ear infections/problems	12	0

*The categories are not mutually exclusive. The same child may be represented in more than one category.

Note: Figures are rounded. Calculations for each row are based on a total of n = 34 for each group.

of time and cost limitations. Half of the children reportedly had not received any treatment for their current health problems.

More index than comparison children in Site 1 had been taken to an emergency room of a hospital or clinic during 1976 (50 versus 38 percent). The group differences were not statistically significant, but they were higher than corresponding figures across Sites 2-5 (32 versus 26 percent). Also, 15 percent of the index children in Site 1 had visited an emergency room in 1976 more than two times. No comparison child had done so. Furthermore, index children were more likely than comparison children to have been taken to an emergency room for both an accident and an illness (23 versus 8 percent) and for such problems as cuts (47 versus 17 percent), bruises (18 versus 8 percent), flu and colds (34 versus 17 percent), and fever (23 versus 17 percent). Group differences on these emergency room variables were either not statistically significant or could not be tested because of small cell frequencies. Approximately 75 percent of both groups of children in Site 1 were taken to a doctor for a checkup in 1976, even when they were not ill, and approximately 60 percent were taken to a physician one or more times for an illness during the same year. Similar figures were reported by parents across Sites 2-5. However, various data from all sites suggest that index children may have received more medical attention than comparison children (including attention in emergency rooms).

According to Site 1 parents, 26 percent of the index and 18 percent of the comparison children had never been to a dentist. This difference between groups was not statistically significant, but the figures for both groups were higher than those reported across Sites 2-5. Approximately 42 percent of the Site 1 children in both groups were taken to a dentist in 1976.

CHILDREN'S PROBLEMS AND UTILIZATION OF OTHER SERVICES

Parents were asked several questions about the mental health status of their target child and abuse and neglect of their child. The letters sent to Site 1 community agencies to validate these parental reports were limited by the fact that only five index parents consented to having their children's names listed on these forms, as discussed in Chapter 1.

Mental Health

All index and 33 comparison parents stated that the three-to-seven-year-old target children had not received any mental health services during 1976. The one remaining comparison parent gave a "don't know" response.

The community validation form from one large mental health facility in Site 1 confirmed these parental reports (although, as noted, only five index names could be included in this survey). This facility served most neighborhoods surveyed.

Two parents, one in each group, did not know if their child had _ever_ received mental health services. All other parents stated that their child had never received these services, and all parents reported their child as not receiving such services at the time of the interview. The testing data presented previously suggest that there may have been emotional and behavioral problems in both groups that were either not perceived or not reported by parents.

Child Abuse and Neglect

One index and one comparison parent reported that their child's name was recorded by an agency or court as an abuse or neglect case in 1976. (All others responded "no.")

The community validation forms did not support the statements of the comparison parents. The one index case reported by an agency may well have been the child reported on by a parent. Limited to only five index names, little can be said about the index group except that a rate of one in five is high (but perhaps unrepresentative). Certainly the comparison rate can be considered high. One agency reported having four of the 34 children in its case load. Another reported having six in its case load. The former was a county agency; the latter was the police. Since, traditionally, police and other public agencies have some working relationships, it is likely that they were reporting on the same group of children, though the authors had no way of checking this supposition.

When asked whether they felt their child was ever a victim of abuse, three index parents (9 percent) and one comparison parent (3 percent) responded affirmatively. According to the comparison parent, this abuse occurred only once. One was reportedly a case of "continuous abuse." In the other two cases, abuse occurred first at ages two and three, the second time at age four, and the third time at age five.

Four index parents and one comparison parent reported their child had been a victim of neglect. (Two of these index parents were among those who reported their child had been a victim of abuse.) For three index children, neglect occurred more than once. In these three cases, respectively, neglect began at ages one, two, and three, and ended at ages two, three, and four. For one index child, the neglect reportedly occurred only once. The neglect of the comparison child was said to begin at age two and end at age five.

From these parents' reports, it appears that at least 9 percent of the index children were abused at some time during their lives and that 12 percent were neglected. Abuse/neglect among the comparison group ranged—according to data from community agencies—from 12 to 18 percent. These figures are four to six times higher than those reported by comparison parents. Abuse and neglect, however, are problems thought to be greatly underreported. Thus, it is likely that these problems were more common among children in this survey than the data indicated. (For further discussion of the problems related to underreporting and to estimating the incidence of abuse and neglect, see Chapter 3.)

Running Away from Home

In Site 1, no responses were expected to the question of whether the child had ever stayed away from home overnight without the parent's permission (the definition of a "runaway" youth used by the

Office of Youth Development, U.S. Department of Health, Education, and Welfare). Surprisingly, two index parents stated that their children were away from home without permission twice at the age of three.

DRUG TREATMENT OF INDEX PARENTS

Reports of Parent Respondents

Only three of the 34 index respondents reported that any member of their family was included in their counseling sessions at their drug treatment program. All such responses pertained to the spouse. One respondent felt that including the spouse in counseling was "very helpful," another rated it as "somewhat helpful," and the third said it was "not helpful at all."

Table 2.17 shows the kinds of services that 23 (68 percent) of

TABLE 2.17

Services Site 1 Index Parents Believe Would Help Their Children and Families

Type of Service	Percentage Responding for Each Item
Counseling sessions that include other family members	52
Drug education for children	26
Recreational activities for clients/families	17
Staff who are more understanding	17
Counseling/psychiatric care for parents and/or children	13
Vocational training and/or help in finding employment	13
Financial help	13
Remove restrictions on attending sessions	13
Strengthen methods of encouraging rehabilitation	13
Other	35

Note: Figures are rounded and based on 23 respondents.

the index respondents believed would be helpful to their child and family if provided by their drug treatment program. Since some respondents listed more than one service, percentages exceed 100. Not shown are the 23 percent who responded "none" (that is, that no services would be helpful) and the 9 percent who either answered "don't know" or refused to answer. Approximately 50 percent of the 23 index respondents believed that counseling sessions that included other family members would be most helpful to their children and family. Drug education for children accounted for the next highest percentage (26) of the responses. Other services that would involve children most directly were recreational services and counseling or psychiatric care.

Reports of Staff of Drug Treatment Programs

In Site 1, 19 parent respondents consented to a questionnaire being sent to their drug treatment program to gather information on them, their families, and the treatment being provided. The two programs in Site 1 completed and returned 16 questionnaires. (One name given by a client could not be identified by program staff. The reasons for a nonresponse on the questionnaires for the other two clients are not known.)

Slightly more than two-thirds of these 16 parents had been enrolled in their present program for two or more years. Five, in fact, had been enrolled for five years or more. Half had been enrolled in drug treatment elsewhere before coming to their present treatment setting, but five of these eight people were enrolled for a year or less in another program.

All 16 parents had been in methadone maintenance while in their current program, eight also had been in methadone detoxification, and one client had been in day treatment.

In 13 cases, program staff had not made any effort to contact members of these clients' families. In one instance, contact occurred because a member of the client's family took the initiative in contacting the program staff. Major reasons given by treatment staff for not contacting family members were clients had not yet requested contact (n = 5), program staff did not make any effort to involve family members in the clients' treatment (n = 3), and clients were not yet at a point in treatment where staff contacted the family (n = 2). An effort was made to contact family members of two clients several months after treatment was initiated.

Staff reported that family members of seven of these 16 clients were involved in treatment in several ways. They were in treatment themselves (n = 4), engaged in social activities at the program (n = 2), and in family counseling (n = 3). In two instances, the clients had been

TABLE 2.18

Goals Set by Drug Treatment Staff for Site 1 Parents

Type of Goal	Percentage Responding for Each Item
Help client become drug free	100
Help client stay on methadone maintenance	46
Help client solve emotional problems	46
Help client with job and/or educational/training needs	69
Help improve family relationships	23
Help improve parental functioning	23

Note: Figures are rounded and based only on reporting respondents (n = 13).

involved in family counseling with their spouses (only) for periods of six months to 1.5 years. Their counselors had at least one year of experience in family counseling. One other client reportedly was receiving family counseling outside the program. The sessions were attended regularly by spouse and children and occasionally by other family members.

Goals that staff had set for 13 of these clients are listed in Table 2.18, together with the percentage of clients to whom each goal applies. As shown, the major goals were to help clients become drug free and obtain a job and/or educational and training needs. Helping clients stay on methadone maintenance and helping them solve their emotional problems were goals for close to 50 percent of these clients.

In five cases, family members shared in the responsibilities for attaining client goals by understanding the client's need for methadone (n = 1), taking the client (spouse) to a community mental health center and the family doctor (n = 1), improving communication in the family (n = 2), and working as a couple with another agency to improve parental functioning (n = 1).

Staff of these programs reported that involving the spouses in the clients' treatment had been "very difficult" in five cases. In two cases, involving the children and the clients' parents and other relatives had also been "very difficult." In six cases, recreational services were provided by the drug treatment program to the clients' children.

In 13 cases, liaisons existed between the drug treatment programs and other community agencies to help meet the needs of these clients. Through liaison arrangements, six clients were being helped by community agencies with employment needs. The same number were being provided medical services, psychiatric services, and help with schooling and/or vocational training.

Community agencies had helped three of these 16 clients obtain housing, three to obtain welfare, one with his probation, one with obtaining emergency food, and one with family planning needs. Two children of these clients had been helped with medical problems, and one had been provided day-care by community agencies through liaison arrangements.

Several clients and/or their children also had been helped by community agencies without liaison relationships between the drug treatment programs and these agencies. For parents, these services had included welfare/public assistance (n = 8), medical services (n = 4), help with employment (n = 3), and help with housing (n = 2). For children, one had been provided medical services and one day-care services.

DISCRIMINANT ANALYSES

A series of 46 simple and multiple discriminant analyses were conducted using variables of interest singly and in various combinations. The tests were conducted on 28 index and 28 comparison families for whom there were complete data on all variables tested.

Table 2.19 depicts the results of a series of simple discriminant analyses conducted for each variable indicated. The variables that discriminate are those that are significant at least at the .05 level.

Table 2.20 shows the results of a series of multiple discriminant analyses of 19 combinations of variables. Based on these analyses, the variables in combination that best discriminate the index and comparison respondents are Stanford-Binet Vocabulary (Mental Age), Bender-Gestalt, medical attention at birth, and the number of emergency room visits in 1976. The criterion used is the highest ratio of F value/Table F value at the .01 level.

An important issue, in view of the significant differences in family income between the index and comparison groups, is the extent to which differences between the two groups are "explained" by income; that is, after income is covaried out, are differences between the index and comparison groups still statistically significant? Table 2.21 shows the results of covariance analysis conducted on the variables of particular interest. The results suggest that income has little effect on "medical attention at birth" and "socioemotional rating." However,

TABLE 2.19

Simple Discriminant Analysis: Site 1

Variable	F	Significance Level[a]
Child's sex	1.78	NS[b]
Child's age	3.19	NS
Birthweight	.15	NS
Medical attention at birth	5.19	.05
Number of emergency room visits, 1976	4.69	.05
Number of visits to M.D., 1976	0	NS
Heroin use during pregnancy	12.79	< .01
Other drug use during pregnancy	12.79	< .01
Spouse helps raise child	.09	NS
Grandparent helps raise child	3.60	NS
Other relative helps raise child	.32	NS
Male head helps support children	.63	NS
Female head helps support children	0	NS
Grandparents/others help support children	1.29	NS
Child supported by public assistance	6.23	.05
Parent's age	.02	NS
Parent's race	.88	NS
Family income	14.74	< .01
Parent employed	7.52	< .01
Parent's years of school	7.20	< .01
Parent arrested	36.00	< .01
Draw-A-Person IQ	6.58	.05
Stanford-Binet Vocabulary (mental age)	13.38	< .01
Peabody Vocabulary	1.58	NS
Bender-Gestalt	9.25	< .01
Socioemotional rating (figure drawings)	9.84	< .01
One-parent family	.88	NS

[a]Significance level is .05.
[b]Not statistically significant.

TABLE 2.20

Multiple Discriminant Analyses

Variable	1	2	3	4	5	6
Birthweight	X[a]					
Medical attention at birth	X					
No. emergency room visits, 1976						
No. visits to M.D., 1976						
Heroin use during pregnancy			X			
Other drug use during pregnancy			X			
Family income						
Parent employed		X				
Parent's education (years of school)		X				
Draw-A-Person IQ				X	X	
Stanford-Binet Vocabulary (mental age)				X	X	
Peabody Vocabulary				X	X	
Bender-Gestalt				X	X	X
Socioemotional rating (figure drawings)				X		X
F	2.8	6.03	10.6	3.71	4.17	7.05
DF	2,53	2,53	2,53	5,50	4,51	2,53
Significance level	NS[b]	<.01	<.01	<.01	<.01	<.01

[a]"X" indicates that the variable is included in the multiple discriminant analysis.

[b]Not statistically significant.

	7	8	9	10	11	12	13	14	15	16	17	18	19
				X	X	X	X	X	X				
				X	X	X			X				
	X	X	X										
		X	X										
	X	X											
									X		X		X
					X	X		X	X	X	X	X	X
						X	X		X	X		X	X
									X			X	
	9.12	6.59	8.58	6.42	9.19	6.89	5.97	8.55	4.77	7.62	6.61	5.61	4.98
	2,53	3,52	2,53	2,53	3,52	4,51	2,53	2,53	6,49	2,53	2,53	3,52	3,52
	<.01	<.01	<.01	<.01	<.01	<.01	<.01	<.01	<.01	<.01	<.01	<.01	<.01

TABLE 2.21

"F" Values before and after Covariance Analysis Controlling for Income: Site 1

Variable	F Test: Before Covariance	F Test: After Covariance
Medical attention at birth	5.19[a]	5.35[a]
Number of emergency room visits, 1976	4.69[a]	2.46
Draw-A-Person IQ	6.58[a]	2.53
Stanford-Binet (mental age)	13.38[b]	4.96[a]
Peabody Vocabulary	1.58	.09
Bender-Gestalt	9.25[b]	4.44[a]
Socioemotional rating (figure drawings)	9.84[b]	8.26[b]

[a]Significant at .05.
[b]Significant at < .01.

income does affect the "Bender-Gestalt" and "Stanford-Binet" variables. (Similar findings on the relationship between income and IQ scores have been reported in many studies.) After covarying out the income, the Stanford-Binet and Bender-Gestalt variables still significantly discriminate between the index and comparison groups (although at the .05 level rather than .01). When income is controlled, "number of emergency room visits in 1976" and "Draw-A-Person IQ" no longer discriminate significantly.

It is concluded that, while family income accounts for some of the variance, the variables with significant F values in Table 2.21 still significantly discriminate between the index and comparison groups.

3

THE EIGHT-TO-SEVENTEEN-YEAR-OLD CHILDREN AND THEIR FAMILIES: SITES 2–5

The principal subjects of this chapter are eight-to-seventeen-year-old children of addicts who resided in four geographically dispersed sites in 1977. These 126 index children, their parents, and an equal number of comparison children and parents provided a great deal of information about themselves and their families during individual interviews lasting from 30 to 45 minutes. Schools also provided information on a subsample of these children, and parents' answers to selected items were "validated" by community service agencies. In addition, a subsample of the target children's three-to-seven-year-old siblings answered questions about themselves and their families in response to the "Robbie the Rabbit" picture interview. The data gathered from these various respondent sources are reported for the four sites combined. The presentation begins with a description of selected characteristics of these parents and their "spouses" (that is, their married and unmarried partners).

BACKGROUND AND CHARACTERISTICS OF PARENTS

Table 3.1 depicts selected characteristics of the parent respondents and their spouses across Sites 2-5.

As shown, more females than males were interviewed. This was related, in part, to the rather high proportion of female-headed households in the index and matched comparison samples. The statistically significant difference ($p = .02$) between groups on this variable is largely caused by the difficulties in finding comparison "matches" for father-only index households and in interviewing comparison fathers in general (see Chapter 1).

TABLE 3.1

Selected Characteristics of Parent Respondents and Spouses: Sites 2-5
(in percentages)

Characteristic	Group	
	Index	Comparison
Sex[a]		
Male	38	24
Female	62	76
Age[b]		
21-25	13	2
26-30	40	10
31-35	25	25
36-40	10	25
41-45	5	12
> 45	6	26
Race/ethnicity[c]		
Black	70	64
White (non-Hispanic)	13	21
Chicano	9	3
Other Latinos	2	5
Other	6	5
Don't know	0	1
Marital status[d]		
Married	42	64
Living with someone	27	2
Living alone	31	33
Respondent's years of education[c]		
< 9	19	19
9-12	62	55
> 12	18	26
Don't know	1	0

(continued)

All the parent respondents were at least 21 years old. The index respondents tended to be younger than the comparison respondents. More than 50 percent were less than 30 years old compared to only 12 percent of the comparison respondents. These age differences were statistically significant ($p < .001$).

TABLE 3.1 (continued)

Characteristic	Group	
	Index	Comparison
Spouse's years of education[c]		
< 9	8	14
9–12	63	52
> 12	21	33
Don't know	8	1
Respondent's employment[c]		
Employed	30	41
Not employed	70	59
Spouse's employment[e]		
Employed	46	73
Not employed	54	27
Family income (1976)[f]		
< $5,000	51	25
$5,000–$7,999	24	14
$8,000–$13,999	16	24
> $13,999	4	35
Don't know/refused	5	3

[a]$\chi^2 = 6$, df = 1, p = .02.
[b]t = 8.1, df = 250, p < .0001.
$\chi^2 = 48.8$, df = 1, p = .001.
[c]Not statistically significant.
[d]$\chi^2 = 12.4$, df = 1, p = .001.
[e]$\chi^2 = 12.5$, df = 1, p = .001.
[f]t = 7.6, df = 250, p < .0001.
$\chi^2 = 21.3$, df = 1, p = .001.
$\chi^2 = 46.6$, df = 3, p < .001.

Note: Figures are rounded. Calculations for each variable on parent respondents are based on n = 126 in each group. Sample sizes for index and comparison spouses/partners are, for education, n = 87 and n = 88, respectively, and, for employment, n = 87 and n = 84.

The families were largely members of minority groups. Of the index respondents, 70 percent were black, 13 percent were white non-Spanish, and 11 percent were either Chicano or of other Latino origins. The figures for the comparison group were similar, and the differences between groups were not statistically significant.

A considerably higher percentage of comparison respondents were married, whereas considerably more index respondents were "living with someone." These differences in marital status were statistically significant ($p = .001$). However, there was no substantial difference between groups in terms of the variable of one- versus two-parent household, as expected, since these "family structure" criteria were used to match comparison households to index households.

The majority of these respondents and their spouses had completed between nine and 12 years of schooling. However, 19 percent of the index respondents did have less than nine years of education, while 18 percent had some education beyond the twelfth grade. The differences between the index and comparison groups on respondents' and spouses' years of education were not statistically significant.

Only about 30 percent of the index respondents were employed. The proportion of comparison respondents employed was not (statistically) significantly different. Comparison spouses were significantly ($p = .001$) more likely to be employed than index spouses.

As might be expected from the employment rates, the index respondents reported generally lower family incomes than did comparison respondents; 51 percent had incomes of less than $5,000 in 1976 compared to 25 percent of the comparison respondents. The difference between the proportion of index and comparison families earning less than $5,000 versus more than $5,000 was statistically significant ($p = .001$). The reported figures represented 1976 income before taxes for all family members and included income from all sources (work, public assistance, unemployment insurance, and so forth).

Table 3.2 summarizes the arrest history of index parents and spouses since the time they assumed a parental role. All arrest data exclude traffic violations. As shown, 56 percent of the index respondents indicated that they had been arrested since becoming a parent compared to 17 percent of the index spouses. Of these index respondents and index spouses, 29 percent and 16 percent, respectively, had been arrested for a drug-related crime. In a few families (5 percent), both the parent figures had been arrested for a drug-related offense. In contrast, only 4 percent of the comparison respondents and 6 percent of their spouses had ever been arrested since becoming a parent. The differences between index and comparison respondent and spouse groups were statistically significant ($p < .001$). (For index and comparison respondents, $\chi^2 = 104.1$, $df = 1$, and for index and comparison spouses, $\chi^2 = 27.8$, $df = 1$.) These data indicate that index parents had been much more involved with the law than had the comparison parents. A similar trend appears for the two groups of target children, as will be shown later in this chapter.

TABLE 3.2

Arrest History of Index Parent Respondents and Spouses: Sites 2-5

	Respondent	Spouse
Ever arrested since becoming a parent*	56%	17%
Drug-related crime	(29%)	(16%)
Nondrug-related crime	(36%)	(23%)
Mean number arrests per arrestee	3.11	5.94

*Excludes traffic violations.

Note: Figures are rounded and based on 126 respondents and 87 spouses.

In keeping with the study design, there was no evidence of drug use among comparison parents and their spouses. Table 3.3 summarizes the drug use history of the index group. In about 5 percent of the index families, the mother had used heroin while pregnant with the target child. Other drugs had been used by 13 percent. Almost 50 percent of the index parent respondents began heroin use before the age of 21, and about 25 percent had had trouble with other drugs since becoming a parent. Also, 37 percent of the spouses reportedly had drug problems since they assumed a parental role. Most (84 percent) of these spouses had received treatment for their drug problem.

In summary, these index families appear to fit most of the social science criteria of "multiproblem" families. This also applies to the comparison group, but to a lesser extent. Provided these demographic and other characteristics, many social scientists, no doubt, would predict poor outcomes among both groups of these children, a prediction that would be correct according to many of the findings described later in this chapter.

The data just presented raise an obvious question: How comparable are the index and comparison families? Selecting the comparison group from the neighborhoods in which index families resided did not lead to equivalency between the groups on rates of employment and family income (as it has in other studies), though equivalency was achieved on race/ethnicity and educational level. Further, while "matching" achieved equivalency in terms of single- versus two-parent households, the marital status of the two groups was significantly different. Two issues are of interest. First, why did these differences occur? And, second, what effect do they have on comparisons between the two groups?

TABLE 3.3

Drug Use History of Index Parent Respondents and Spouses: Sites 2-5

Drug Use Variables	Percentage
Drug use of mother during pregnancy with target child (n = 126)[a]	
Heroin	5
Other drugs[b]	13
Age respondent began heroin use (n = 126)	
< 16	10
16-17	11
18-20	24
21-25	29
26-31	17
> 31	6
Don't know	3
Respondent with other drug problems since becoming a parent (n = 126)	24
Spouse with drug problems since becoming a parent (n = 87)	37
Spouse received treatment for drug problem since becoming a parent (n = 32)	84

[a]Categories are not mutually exclusive.

[b]Includes use of such drugs as marijuana, barbiturates, amphetamines, cocaine, and "other drugs" several times a week "for at least one month" during pregnancy.

Note: Figures are rounded.

The differences between groups in terms of marital status may be a reflection of different life-styles among people who are or have been heroin addicts. Descriptions of addicts' life-styles often indicate rather low proportions of individuals who are living with legal spouses (Sowder 1977). It can only be said that the two groups did not differ significantly in terms of representing a single-parent household. The quality of their relationships with spouses or partners cannot be determined from the information collected. However, it is worth noting that only 2 percent of the comparison group had unmarried partners compared to 27 percent of the index group. These unmarried partners had been living in the index households only an average of three years.

(The average was similar for unmarried partners in the comparison group.) This finding suggests that there has been considerable instability in those index households in which there was an unmarried partner.

Differences between spouse groups in employment may be attributable to the larger number of male spouses in the comparison group. Males generally can be expected to experience a higher employment rate than females. Further, since unemployment rates are high nationwide among both male and female addicts (Burt, Glynn, and Sowder 1979), it is hardly surprising to find high unemployment rates in these index households. Having a criminal justice system record, as did many in the index group, is also a well-recognized barrier to employment.

Because fewer index than comparison respondents and spouses were employed, it is not surprising that index families reported lower incomes than did comparison families. The high proportion of comparison families having more than a $13,999 income in 1976 was at least partially attributable to there being two employed people in the comparison households.

A further issue is that of the extent to which these differences might act to bias comparisons between the index and comparison groups. As explained fully later in this chapter, none of these variables (except not living with a legal spouse) is related to any other variable analyzed by factor analysis. The factor analysis shows that age of parent, parent's employment, and family income correlate only with each other. They are not correlated with any other study variables and do not enter any of the factors except the factor they comprise. Therefore, it does not appear that these differences should distort comparisons between the two groups.

FAMILY STRUCTURE

It has already been noted that index and comparison households differed significantly in terms of the marital status of the parents but not in terms of being single-parent families. Some degree of family instability had obviously occurred in about one-third of each group represented by single-parent households. However, the short average length of stay of unmarried partners in another 27 percent of the index group suggests there was much more family instability among index households. Overall, the mean length of residence of spouses in index households was about nine years. The comparable figure for the comparison group was about 18 years. However, these average differences may be partly attributable to the fact that comparison parents were an older group.

TABLE 3.4

Parent's Expectations of Child on Different Tasks by Age: Sites 2-5
(in percentages)

	Age of Child																			
	< 1		1		2		3-6		7-10		11-12		13-15		> 16		Don't Know		Total	
Task	I	C	I	C	I	C	I	C	I	C	I	C	I	C	I	C	I	C	I	C
Feed him/herself	18	16	39	43	32	36	8	5	0	0	0	0	1	0	0	0	0	0	100	100
Be toilet trained	13	10	32	30	44	53	10	6	0	0	0	0	0	0	0	0	1	0	100	99
Help around the house	0	0	2	1	5	7	47	45	42	41	3	2	0	2	1	1	0	1	100	100
Have a part-time job	0	0	0	0	0	0	0	0	3	2	10	13	45	47	37	36	4	1	100	100
Have a full-time job	0	0	0	0	0	0	0	0	0	0	1	0	3	2	67[a]	86[a]	29[b]	11[b]	100	99
Stay alone in the house	0	0	0	0	0	0	0	0	13	7	25	17	36	37	22	32	4	6	100	99
Decide how late he/she can stay out at night	0	0	0	0	0	0	0	0	0	0	3	3	6	7	72[c]	83[c]	18[d]	6[d]	101	100
Take care of younger children when parents are away	0	0	0	0	0	0	[e]	0	9	4	25	18	38	40	25	33	3	4	100	99

[a] $\chi^2 = 11.7$, df = 1, $p < .001$.
[b] $\chi^2 = 12$, df = 1, $p < .001$.
[c] $\chi^2 = 4.5$, df = 1, $p = .05$.
[d] $\chi^2 = 8.3$, df = 1, $p = .01$.
[e] Less than 1 percent.

Note: Figures are rounded and are based in each row on n = 126 in each group.

Both the index and comparison families appear to have had substantial ties with extended family members. The children's grandparents or other relatives lived in 21 percent of the index and 26 percent of the comparison households at least nine months out of the year at the time of interview.

Index parents tended to have slightly fewer children under 19 than did comparison parents (an average of 3.5 versus 3.7) probably because they were a younger group. Of the 437 index youngsters under age 19, 96 percent were living within the household at the time of interview, compared to 99 percent of the 467 comparison youngsters. Most children not living with parent respondents were with their other parent or with a relative. There were no children in foster care.

Among the eight-to-seventeen-year-old target children, about two-thirds in each group were female, and about 75 percent were between the ages of eight and 12. Group differences on these variables were not statistically significant.

CHILD-REARING PRACTICES, PARENTAL EXPECTATIONS, AND FAMILY VALUES AND INTERACTIONS

Parent respondents were asked a number of questions about their child-rearing practices, their hopes and expectations of their children, and family interactions. The eight-to-seventeen-year-old target children were also asked about their perceptions of their parents' expectations and hopes for them, their families' values, and about activities that they shared with other family members. In addition, the three-to-seven-year-old siblings were queried in a few of the same areas through the Robbie the Rabbit picture interview.

Parent respondents in both groups reported similar beliefs about the age a child should be before performing certain tasks. Few statistically significant differences were found (see Table 3.4). Comparison parents were significantly more likely to say a child should be age 16 or older before having a full-time job and deciding how late to stay out at night ($p < .001$). On these two questions, index parents were significantly more likely to respond "don't know," a finding that suggests they may have given little thought, as yet, to these aspects of child rearing. Other findings were not statistically significant. About 60 percent of the parents in both groups reportedly believed a child should be able to feed himself before the age of two, and about 40 percent thought a child should be toilet trained before age two. Around 45 percent of all parents thought a child could help around the house by ages three to six. However, almost as many felt the child should be aged seven to ten before doing so. By around age 11 or 13, most parents seemed to feel a child could stay alone in the house and

TABLE 3.5

Parental Hopes and Expectations for Child: Sites 2-5
(in percentages)

Thing Child Might Do in Future	Index		Comparison	
	Like	Expect	Like	Expect
Finish high school	88	78	80	67
Go to college	89	50	80	39
Get some vocational training	40	27	41	29
Get married	56	53	47	43
Become a good parent	70[a]	58[b]	58[a]	40[b]
Make a lot of money	55[c]	23	36[c]	15
Have a career in military service	17	5	9	8
Have a career in sports	33	18	17	11
Have a "helping career"	41	28	41	20

[a] $\chi^2 = 3.9$, df = 1, p = .05.
[b] $\chi^2 = 8.5$, df = 1, p = .01.
[c] $\chi^2 = 8.4$, df = 1, p = .01.

Note: Figures are rounded and are based in each row on n = 126 in each group.

take care of younger children when parents were away. Most parents felt children were old enough to have a part-time job somewhere between the ages of 13 and 16.

When asked what they would "like" their children to do, parents in both groups reportedly had high hopes for their children in terms of education, marriage, parenthood, and financial success. Expectations of children in these areas are lower than parental desires, as might be expected (see Table 3.5). However, index parents were significantly more likely than comparison parents to both want and expect their child to become a good parent (p = .05 and p = .01, respectively) and significantly more likely to want their child to make a lot of money (p = .01).

The high value parents placed on their child's finishing high school and going to college appeared to be well understood by the eight-to-seventeen-year-old target children (see Table 3.6). In fact, more children than parents stated that the parents wanted and expected them to finish high school or would like for them to go to college. The children also felt that education was important to them. No statistically significant differences were found between index and comparison groups on any variables related to the future education of the target children.

Both groups of parents were likely to rely on oral methods (for example, talks, lectures, "yelling at" the children) to discipline their children (see Table 3.7). Physical punishment was reportedly "never" used by about 50 percent of the parents in both groups. Among the remainder of the parents, reliance on physical punishment was restricted mostly to "once in a while." About two-thirds of the parents relied, at least occasionally, on some form of deprivation (for example, setting the child in a chair or sending him to his room). The differences between index and comparison parents in disciplinary practices were not statistically significant. Nor were the differences between parent groups on setting rules about what the children should eat or punishing them for disobeying rules about eating (see Table 3.8). These rules reportedly existed in 46 percent of the index and 43 percent of the comparison homes. Denying a food the child wanted

TABLE 3.6

Responses of Eight to Seventeen Year Olds to Statements about Family Values and Education/Achievement
(percentages responding "true" across sites)

Statement	Index	Comparison
It's okay with my family if I don't finish school.	8	5
My family would like me to go to college.	93	90
Making good grades in school is important in my family.	97	98
My family expects me to always do my best.	94	100

Note: Figures are rounded and are based in each row on n = 126 in each group.

TABLE 3.7

Use and Extent of Different Disciplinary Practices by Parents: Sites 2-5 (in percentages)

Type of Discipline	Daily		3-4 Times a Week		Once in a While		Never		Total	
	I	C	I	C	I	C	I	C	I	C
Send to room or set in chair	5	4	14	7	46	58	34	31	99	100
Slap or hit with hand	2	0	4	3	45	48	50	48	101	99
Talk to or lecture	31	29	32	24	36	43	2	4	101	100
Yell at	33	22	17	13	36	48	14	7	100	100
Take away privilege (e.g., television)	2	1	2	7	69	63	28	29	101	100
Whip with belt, switch, object	2	0	4	2	43	40	51	57	100	99
Threaten with whipping	18	13	14	12	46	42	22	32	100	99

Note: Figures are rounded. Calculations in each row are based on n = 125 index and n = 126 comparison children. Total n's less than 126 in the index group represent "refuse to answer." There was one "refused to answer" in the index group for each item.

TABLE 3.8

Punishments for Disobeying Rules about Eating as Reported by Parents across Sites 2-5 (percentages responding "yes")

Type of Punishment	Index	Comparison
Child is denied a wanted food (e.g., dessert)	44	46
Spank/whip	5	6
Nothing	10	19
Make child sit until food is finished	10	7
Take away something child wants (e.g., going out)	16	7
Give lecture on why food must be eaten*	9	4
Other	7	11
Total	101	100

*Response given to an "other" category in the questionnaire.

Note: Figures are rounded and based on 58 index and 54 comparison respondents.

(for example, dessert) was the most frequently reported punishment for disobeying rules about eating.

According to approximately 90 percent of the 45 index and 49 comparison siblings of the target children, parents usually told them to to eat all the food on their plates. Of the index and comparison siblings, 40 percent and 53 percent, respectively, said they would not get punished for not eating what they were told to eat. Of those who said they would get punished, 50 percent of the index and 39 percent of the comparison siblings said they would get "spanked" for disobeying. Most of the rest said they would be sent to their room for disobeying. Group differences were not statistically significant on these variables.

When asked how strict they were in rearing their children, index parents were more likely than comparison parents to say they were "not strict at all" (17 versus 8 percent), and they were less likely to report themselves as being "very strict" (9 versus 13 percent). These group differences were not statistically significant. Although 75 percent or more of the target children in both groups felt children in their families had to obey a lot of rules and would get punished for disobeying rules, fewer index than comparison children perceived their families as having a lot of rules (74 versus 82 percent), and fewer said they would get punished for disobeying rules (78 versus 82 percent). These findings were consistent with the parents' reports. Differences between the child groups were not statistically significant on these variables.

In summary, index and comparison parents were very similar in disciplinary practices. However, it is worth noting that there was a consistent trend of more permissive child-rearing practices among the index group.

Of the index parents and comparison parents, 41 percent and 34 percent, respectively, reported that they either did not raise their children the way their parents raised them or did so only "a little." This difference was statistically significant ($\chi^2 = 10$, df = 1, p = .05). However, the majority of parents in both groups said they raised their children "a lot" or "some" like their parents raised them. This suggests that continuity across generations in child rearing was more often the "rule" than the "exception" among these families, as it is reportedly in most societies (Sowder 1972).

Index parents were less likely than comparison parents to state that they spend 12 hours or more with their child each week (68 versus 83 percent). This difference was statistically significant ($\chi^2 = 8$, df = 1, p = .01). Since 24 percent of the index parents said their drug use made them unable to spend enough time with their children, addiction may be related to this phenomenon. But other factors may also account for the fact that index parents spent less time with their children. One factor, as reported by target children, was that people in index families were significantly more likely to stay out at night and sleep late during the day than were people in comparison households (32 versus 17 percent; $\chi^2 = 7.6$, df = 1, p = .01). Also, though group differences were not statistically significant, female heads of household of index families were more likely than their comparison counterparts to be involved in the financial support of their children (43 versus 32 percent), a fact that would tend to lessen the time mothers could spend with their children.

Reports by the target children did not suggest that index children were more deprived of family companionship than comparison children (though questions on this dimension did not distinguish the addict parent respondent from other family members). Data reported by target children suggested that index families were significantly less affectionate than comparison families in terms of "hugging and kissing a lot." Compared to 69 percent of the comparison children, 53 percent of the index children answered "true" to the statement "We hug and kiss a lot in this family" ($\chi^2 = 6.67$, df = 1, p = .01). However, no statistically significant differences appeared between the target groups on such variables as fighting a lot within the family (which reportedly

TABLE 3.9

Types of People Helping to Raise and Financially Support the Eight-to-Seventeen-Year-Old Children (in percentages)

Type of Person/Agency	Index	Comparison
Helping to raise child		
Spouse/partner	62	71
Child's grandparents	62[a]	16[a]
Other relatives	18[b]	11[b]
Child's older siblings	9[c]	24[c]
Friends/neighbors/others	12	10
Providing financial support		
Male household head	49[d]	65[d]
Female household head	43	32
Child's grandparents	23[e]	5[e]
Other relatives	13	5
Welfare/public assistance	63[f]	39[f]

[a] $\chi^2 = 56.2$, df = 1, p = .001.
[b] $\chi^2 = 8.3$, df = 1, p = .01.
[c] $\chi^2 = 9.2$, df = 1, p = .01.
[d] $\chi^2 = 6.5$, df = 1, p < .05.
[e] $\chi^2 = 15.7$, df = 1, p = .001.
[f] $\chi^2 = 15.3$, df = 1, p = .001.

Note: Figures are rounded. Calculations on each item are based on n = 126 in each group.

characterized only a few families); wanting to tell parents about accomplishments or problems (as almost all children did); engaging in activities together, including watching television, eating dinner, shopping, and other activities (which the majority of these family members did frequently); going to religious services often (as 56 percent of the index and 68 percent of the comparison families did); or being separated from their families for a month or more (which occurred in about 25 percent of each group of these families). The reports of the target children on family interactions were generally supported by the reports of their three-to-seven-year-old siblings. These siblings reported frequent family interactions (for example, playing games, eating dinner together). The one outstanding (but not statistically significant) difference between the sibling groups was that a higher percentage of comparison than index siblings said they would rather eat dinner with their family than alone (84 versus 73 percent).

Index target children were significantly more likely than comparison children to report that family members visited friends and relatives together often; 45 versus 27 percent of each group did so daily or at least several times a week ($\chi^2 = 9$, df = 1, p = .01). This finding supported other data that suggested that index families relied more heavily than did comparison families on an extended family network (see Table 3.9). The index children's grandparents and "other relatives" were significantly (p = .001 and .01, respectively) more likely than their comparison counterparts to be involved in helping to "raise" the children. Index grandparents were also significantly (p = .001) more likely to be providing financial support for these children, as were welfare/public assistance agencies (p = .001). On the other hand, male heads of household of index families were significantly (p = .05) less likely than their comparison counterparts to be providing financial support for the target children.

About two-thirds of the index parents did report that their drug use interfered with their being the "kind of parent they would like to be." Among many of these 79 parents, their drug use had reportedly made them unable to provide a better financial situation for their children (40 percent) and/or spend enough time with their children (38 percent). Some also reported their drug use had made them "emotionally unfit" to be the kind of parent they would like to be (20 percent), unable to provide proper care for the child (15 percent), and/or unable to hold a job (10 percent).

CHILDREN'S FRIENDSHIP PATTERNS AND ACTIVITIES

The information supplied by parents and children indicated that over 90 percent of the eight-to-seventeen-year-old children in both groups generally had more than one friend and that their parents had met a lot of these friends. In about two-thirds of the cases, these friends visited the homes of target children daily or several times a week. During these visits, the children were most likely to spend their time watching television or playing cards and games (83 percent of each group) or sports (48 percent of the index and 40 percent of the comparison children). In only 6 percent of each group did the children spend a lot of time "hanging around on the streets." The differences between the index and comparison groups on these variables were not statistically significant.

Index parents were significantly more likely than comparison parents to disapprove of some of the target children's friends (60 versus 38 percent; $\chi^2 = 11$, df = 2, $p < .01$). However, many of the parents in both groups did not report any such disapproval (40 percent and 62 percent of the index and comparison parents, respectively).

According to the teachers of 46 index and 49 comparison target youngsters, index children were more likely than comparison children to either have "a lot" of friends (23 versus 12 percent) or "no friends" (35 versus 27 percent). However, differences were not statistically significant.

Among the three-to-seven-year-old siblings of the target children, most perceived themselves as making friends easily. This was slightly less true for index than comparison siblings (71 versus 84 percent). Also, 18 percent of these 45 index siblings, as compared to 4 percent of the 49 comparison siblings, said they would rather play alone than with a lot of friends. This difference was not statistically significant.

Despite the similarity between index and comparison children in friendship patterns, a consistent trend did emerge; namely, a higher proportion of the index group appeared to be "loners." According to parents and teachers, about 9 percent of the index target children had no friends, compared to about 3 percent of the comparison children. Also, as noted, index siblings were more likely than comparison siblings to prefer playing alone. This "loner" trait appeared also among the Site 1 index children. The trait has been reported among adult addicts (Sowder 1977) and, therefore, may be a life-style that some of these children had learned from their parents.

CHILDREN'S PERCEPTIONS OF THEMSELVES AND OTHERS

For reasons not clarified in the data collection, a substantial proportion (47 to 55 percent) of the eight-to-seventeen-year-old index children consistently rated themselves "much better" than others their own age on such things as being good in sports, being well-dressed, being good-looking, having teachers like them, having many friends their own age, and being able to defend themselves. Comparison children were more likely than index children to rate themselves as "a little better" than others their own age on these same statements.

Few children in either group rated themselves as "worse" than others. Group differences were not statistically significant.

True-false responses to another item indicated that about 85 percent of the eight-to-seventeen-year-old children in both groups felt good about themselves almost all of the time. However, 50 percent of the children in both groups reported that they often felt bored, about two-thirds worried about what others thought of them, about one-third often felt lonesome and sad, and approximately 60 percent said they usually kept their anger to themselves. Index children were more likely than comparison children to answer "true" to the statement "I get into a lot of fights" (19 versus 10 percent). None of these differences between groups was statistically significant. However, the index group was significantly more likely than the comparison group to answer two statements in ways that indicated an external locus of control (Rotter 1966); that is, they were significantly more likely to answer "false" to the statement "When I get into trouble it is usually my own fault" (46 versus 30 percent; $\chi^2 = 6.3$, df = 1, $p < .05$) and "true" to the statement "I think good luck is more important than hard work for success" (44 versus 31 percent; $\chi^2 = 4.5$, df = 1, $p < .05$). Since adult addicts reportedly score high on measures denoting an external locus of control (for example, DeLeon 1974; Obitz and Oziel 1973), it is possible that the index children had learned this orientation from their parents.

Like their older brothers and sisters, most three-to-seven-year-old siblings also appeared to have a positive self-image. Responses of the sibling groups indicated that nearly all of these children identified with the picture of Robbie who looked pleased and proud of himself. Speaking of themselves, the children often said they liked the "way they looked" or they liked themselves because of something they had done. When these responses were grouped into "values/feelings about self" (for example, personal appearance, feeling "happy," feeling "good about" self) as opposed to "achievement oriented" accomplishments (for example, good at games, good in school), index siblings were significantly more likely than comparison siblings to report liking themselves because of some "achievement-oriented" reason (54 versus 29 percent; $\chi^2 = 5.3$, df = 1, $p < .05$). These data suggest that there may be different reasons for the underlying positive self-concept in each sibling group.

Viewing Robbie the Rabbit in a deep hole being offered a helping hand by a strange grown-up, index siblings were significantly more likely than their comparison peers to say Robbie would give his hand to the strange grown-up in order to get out of the hole (82 versus 61 percent; $\chi^2 = 5$, df = 1, $p < .05$). But they were only slightly more likely to say they would give their own hand to a strange grown-up if they were in Robbie's predicament (62 versus 57 percent). Among those who said they would not give their hand to a strange grown-up, index siblings were more likely than comparison siblings to say they would not do so because they would want to try to get out of the hole themselves (75 versus 45 percent), whereas comparison children were more likely to indicate being afraid of a strange grown-up (55 versus 25 percent). Although the data were not conclusive and the differences between groups not statistically significant or not tested because of small cell frequencies, the results suggested that index siblings may have had more trust in strange adults than did comparison siblings. It is also worth noting that index siblings tended to give an "achievement-oriented" response to why they would give their hand to a strange grown-up. This was consistent with the responses they gave for liking themselves.

Despite the achievement orientation noted among index siblings, there were no statistically significant differences between the two groups of siblings in response to a picture that denoted persistence at a difficult task (a factor highly correlated with school achievement). Of the index and comparison siblings, 55 percent and 65 percent, respectively, said they would keep on working at a hard task. Reasons given included "I want to see what it looks like," "I like to try," and "I like to make things." One reason, however, was given by only one index sibling as compared to 14 comparison siblings, namely, "I want to finish it."

CHILDREN AT WORK

The few inquiries made of the eight-to-seventeen-year-old children about their work indicated that almost all of the index and comparison children had chores to do around the house and that 56 percent of the children in both groups were expected to do these chores daily. Considerable proportions of the children in both groups got paid for doing chores at home, for doing chores for neighbors, and for baby-sitting. Index children were more likely than comparison children to earn money by doing chores in their homes (55 versus 48 percent) and by baby-sitting (46 versus 36 percent), but these differences were not statistically significant. Five (4 percent) of the index children did report that they earned money by doing things that could get them in trouble with the police. This was not reported by any comparison children.

Most of the 16 index and 22 comparison youngsters aged 14 to 17 were paid for doing chores at home. In addition, 59 percent of the 16 index and 41 percent of their comparison peers were employed at various types of jobs (for example, work in restaurants, offices, and so forth). About 82 percent of these teenagers reported that they used their earnings to buy things they needed or wanted, and slightly over 50 percent spent their earnings "for fun." Some of these earnings were saved by about 69 percent of these teenagers. However, the index teenagers were more likely than their comparison peers to use some of their earnings to help support their families (56 versus 32 percent). These group differences in employment and spending/saving habits were either not statistically significant or were not tested because of small cell frequencies.

SCHOOL STATUS

At the time of interview, approximately 70 percent of the index and 68 percent of the comparison eight-to-seventeen-year-old children were enrolled in grades one through six, 15 to 17 percent of each respective group were in grades seven through eight, and most of the rest were in grades nine through 12. According to parents, six of the 126 index target children and three comparison children were not in school. None of the children had graduated from school. None of these group differences in school status was statistically significant.

Parents and target children provided somewhat different answers to the question of the approximate number of school days the children had missed for various reasons. About 10 percent of the children in both groups said they had not missed any school days during the year because of sickness or because they were kept home by their parents. Corresponding figures from parents were higher (16 percent of the index and 20 percent of the comparison parents). The differences between comparison parents and children were statistically significant ($\chi^2 = 5.5$, df = 1, $p < .05$). The majority of parents and children in both groups reported that no school days were missed because the children "skipped/didn't want to do" or because they were "told not to come by school staff." However, missing school for these two reasons occurred more often in the index group. School was missed because the child "skipped" or didn't want to go according to 18 percent of the index parents and 26 percent of the index children. Corresponding figures for the comparison parents and children were 6 and 16 percent. Only the differences between comparison parents and children were statistically significant ($\chi^2 = 5.6$, df = 1, $p < .05$). About 17 percent of both the index parent and child groups said school was missed because the children were told "not to come by school staff." Corresponding figures for comparison parents and children were 9 and 6 percent.

Approximately 50 percent of the parents in each group reported that their children were doing "very well" on most school subjects. Most of the remaining parents said their children were doing "fair" on most subjects. About two-thirds of the children in both groups had won some awards or honors in school. Index youngsters were more likely than comparison youngsters to have won awards for sports (20 versus 12 percent), while the comparison youngsters were more likely to have won types of academic or school-achievement honors. For example, 25 percent of the comparison children compared to 15 percent of the index children were honor students. About the same proportions in each group had won honors in a specific subject area.

As is noted in Table 3.10, index parents were significantly ($p < .05$) more likely than comparison parents to have been contacted by the schools because of their child's misconduct (31 versus 19 percent). They were also more likely to have been contacted because their child had been absent from school (17 versus 9 percent). However, according to the eight-to-seventeen-year-old children, index parents were significantly more likely than comparison parents to like the child's teachers "a lot" (58 versus 44 percent; $\chi^2 = 11.7$, $df = 3$, $p < .01$). Almost 90 percent of all target children reported liking their teachers "a lot" or "some," 63 percent of the index and 58 percent of the comparison children liked their teachers "a lot," and 72 and 60 percent of the respective groups liked school "a lot." The reports of the siblings were similar. Of the index and comparison siblings, 89 percent and 96 percent, respectively, felt "happy" about school and/or about going to school. None of these differences was statistically significant.

The eight-to-seventeen-year-old index children were somewhat more likely than their comparison counterparts to perceive themselves as either being at the very "center of things going on at school" (17 versus 15 percent) or at an extreme distance away from the center (22 versus 14 percent). Many children in both groups were further away from the "center" than they would like to be. Further, there were statistically significant differences ($p < .01$) in the "difference scores" <u>within</u> each group in terms of where the children were as opposed to where they wanted to be. Values from the t tests indicated that children in both groups generally were not where they would prefer to be. Differences <u>between</u> groups in difference scores were not statistically significant.

A few of the target children were receiving services from their schools at the time of interview. According to their parents, index youngsters were more likely than comparison children to be receiving free meals (7 versus 2 percent), counseling (16 versus 12 percent), and individual help with school subjects (20 versus 15 percent) but were less likely to be receiving special education (7 versus 11 percent) and "programs to help them catch up" (14 versus 25 percent). These differences either were not statistically significant or were not tested because of small cell frequencies. When asked if they had

TABLE 3.10

School Problems of Eight-to-Seventeen-Year-Old Children (in percentages)

School Problem	Index	Comparison
Absenteeism (parents' reports)		
Child ill/parent kept home	84	80
Child skipped/didn't want to go[a]	18	6
Child told not to come by school staff[a]	5	3
Parent contacted by school for absences[a]	17	9
	(n = 120)	(n = 123)
Missed six or more days (teachers' reports)	85[b]	55[b]
	(n = 46)	(n = 49)
Behavior problems		
Parent contacted by school for child's	31[c]	19[c]
misbehavior (parents' reports)	(n = 120)	(n = 123)
Needs discipline (teachers' reports)	71[d]	45[d]
	(n = 40)	(n = 41)
Child doesn't obey teacher	49[e]	11[e]
(teachers' reports)	(n = 39)	(n = 44)
Child doesn't work well in groups	54[f]	34[f]
(teachers' reports)	(n = 39)	(n = 44)
Child destructive of school property[a]	15	4
(teachers' reports)	(n = 39)	(n = 44)
Received counseling for fighting	32	19
(children's reports)[g]	(n = 34)	(n = 23)
Received tutoring/special education	35[h]	23[h]
(children's reports)	(n = 120)	(n = 123)
Repeated grades (teachers' reports)	24	7
	(n = 45)	(n = 46)
Received counseling	28	19
(children's reports)	(n = 120)	(n = 123)

[a]Small cell sizes prohibited statistical testing.
[b]$\chi^2 = 9.8$, df = 1, $p = .01$.
[c]$\chi^2 = 4.1$, df = 1, $p < .05$.
[d]$\chi^2 = 5.6$, df = 1, $p < .05$.
[e]$\chi^2 = 14$, df = 1, $p < .001$.
[f]$\chi^2 = 3.3$, df = 1, $p < .05$.
[g]Includes only those who received some type of counseling in school.
[h]$\chi^2 = 4.4$, df = 1, $p < .05$.

ever received tutoring at school, a significantly ($p < .05$) higher proportion of index than comparison children responded affirmatively (35 versus 23 percent). More index children also reported receiving counseling services (28 versus 19 percent), but this difference was not statistically significant (see Table 3.10). Among this subsample, more index than comparison children had received counseling for "fighting" (32 versus 19 percent). Small cell sizes prohibited statistical testing on this variable.

Teachers reporting on 46 index and 49 comparison children (see Table 3.10) were significantly ($p < .01$) more likely to say that index children needed to be disciplined for misbehavior (71 percent of the index group versus 45 percent of the comparison group). School failures were also higher among index than comparison children in this subsample (24 versus 7 percent). For index children, reasons for repeating grades, when given, were more likely to be academic failure and absenteeism. According to teachers, index youngsters were also significantly ($p = .01$) more likely than comparison children to have missed six or more days of school (66 versus 45 percent). "Family-related" problems were more likely to be reported as reasons for the index children's absences than for those of their comparison peers.

However, in terms of current academic standing, index target children were only slightly more likely than the comparison children to be in the "lower third" of their class (35 versus 31 percent), and a slightly higher proportion were in the "upper third" (33 versus 31 percent), according to their teachers. These differences were not statistically significant.

Teachers reported that index children were significantly less likely than comparison children to "obey the teachers" (51 versus 89 percent—$p < .001$) or to work well in groups (46 versus 66 percent—$p < .05$) (see Table 3.10). They were also somewhat less likely to work well alone (54 versus 59 percent) and to enjoy learning (59 versus 67 percent) but somewhat more likely to follow instructions well (61 versus 59 percent). The last three differences were not statistically significant. About 15 percent of these index youngsters were reportedly destructive of school property and/or destructive in the classroom. These behaviors were reported for only 4 percent of the comparison children. Index children were also significantly more likely than comparison children to be rated by their teachers as being "below average in popularity with other students" (34 versus 17 percent; $\chi^2 = 4.3$, df = 1, $p = .05$).

According to teachers, a greater percentage of index children ($n = 45$) than comparison children ($n = 49$) needed special services from the school (42 versus 28 percent). They were also more likely to be perceived as needing individual mental health counseling (46

TABLE 3.11

Number of Children Provided or Needing Special Types of School Resources As Reported by Teachers across Sites 2-5 (in percentages)

Special Resource/Service	Provided I	Provided C	Needed but Not Provided* I	Needed but Not Provided* C
Remedial reading (general)	22	12	4	2
Remedial reading (special subject areas)	9	9	9	2
For slow learners	7	13	4	2
For the gifted	7	4	0	0
Speech therapy	4	0	4	0
For emotionally disturbed	2	4	4	0
For orthopedically handicapped	0	0	2	0
For mentally retarded	0	0	2	0
Other	0	4	0	0

*Not provided for various reasons, for example, not available or overcrowded classes.

Note: Figures are rounded. Calculations for each category/group are based on 45 index and 47 comparison children.

versus 26 percent), family counseling (37 versus 26 percent), and protective services (15 versus 4 percent). Only the difference in the perceived need for individual mental health counseling was statistically significant ($\chi^2 = 3.4$, df = 1, $p < .05$).

In summary, various respondent sources indicated that the index target children had more school-related problems than had their comparison peers. Several of these problems are resummarized in Table 3.10. Some of these problems, according to teachers, required special services or resources from the schools. The scant data collected from teachers suggest that there generally were more index than comparison children who needed, but were not provided, special services by the schools (see Table 3.11). Why this was so cannot be determined from the information collected.

PHYSICAL HEALTH STATUS OF TARGET CHILDREN AND UTILIZATION OF MEDICAL SERVICES

The reported incidence of low birthweight (about 19 percent in both groups) considerably exceeds the 1975 figures for the general population (7.4 percent) and for blacks (13.1 percent) (U.S. Department of Health, Education, and Welfare 1975). Since low birthweight is correlated with later learning disorders (Sowder 1977), this small group of youngsters may be at unusually high risk in terms of school achievement. Prematurity rates were similar to the low birthweight rates (15 and 17 percent, respectively, for the index and comparison groups). The same percentage (13) of youngsters in both groups required medical services at birth for various disorders (for example, prematurity, heart conditions, and respiratory conditions).

Index parents were significantly more likely than comparison parents to rate the current health of their children as either "excellent" or "fair-poor" ($\chi^2 = 7.9$, df = 2, $p < .05$). However, index children were significantly less likely than their parents to rate their health as "excellent" ($\chi^2 = 10.5$, df = 2, $p < .01$). (Similar discrepancies between parents and children in ratings of the child's health status occurred in the National Health Survey, 1966-70.) Comparison children were significantly more likely than their eight-to-seventeen-year-old index peers to rate their health as "excellent" (59 versus 40 percent; $\chi^2 = 10.6$, df = 2, $p < .01$).

The percentages of parents in each group who rated the child's health as "fair-poor" were at least twice as high as the corresponding figures (3.6) in the National Health Survey, 1966-70 (U.S. Department of Health, Education, and Welfare 1975). The high percentage (15) of index parents who rated their child's health as "fair-poor" also exceeded the percentage (6.3) of black parents who gave this rating in the national survey. These data, then, suggest that a sizable proportion of the index parents did not perceive their child to be in the best of health.

One of the health problems reported by parents rating their child's health as "fair-poor" was asthma. Of the index parents, 16 percent reported their target children had "asthma," compared to only 2 percent of the index children. On the other hand, no comparison parent gave this response, but 10 percent of the comparison children reported having asthma. Dental problems among target children were reported by 20 percent of the index parents. No comparison parents gave this response. Perhaps this difference partly reflects the more dire economic straits among index families. Hearing/ear problems (10 versus 12 percent of the index and comparison children), emotional problems (15 versus 37 percent of the index and comparison children), and several "other" problems were also reported. Approximately one-third of the index children and 25 percent of the comparison children in "fair-poor" health were reportedly not receiving any medical services for these health problems.

Current health problems were reported by 33 percent of the index children and 39 percent of the comparison children. The mean number of problems reported per child was 1.4. Colds, flu, and so forth, accounted for a sizable proportion of the problems. Other problems included headaches, stomach aches, asthma, urinary problems, and dizziness/blackouts. Group differences were not statistically significant. The seriousness of these problems cannot be determined from the data.

In 1976, 26 percent of the index target children and 25 percent of the comparison children were reportedly taken to the emergency room of a hospital or clinic. Group differences were not statistically significant with regard to the number of visits. Most children experienced only one or two visits. Accidents were the most commonly reported reasons for emergency room visits (60 versus 33 percent of the index and comparison group visits, respectively, were attributed to accidents). Illnesses, such as flu, fever, and allergic reactions, accounted for most of the remaining visits.

Approximately 60 percent of the children in both groups had reportedly visited a doctor for a checkup in 1976 at least once, according to parents. Moreover, according to parents, approximately half of these children were taken to a doctor for an illness in 1976. Figures supplied by the children on checkups were significantly higher than those reported by parents in both groups ($\chi^2 = 27$, df = 4, p = .0001). Possibly some children were including physical examinations received in school, which were not reported by parents.

According to parents, 19 percent of the index and 12 percent of the comparison children had never been to a dentist. The figure reported by index parents is higher than the figure (11.6) reported by parents in the National Health Survey, 1966-70 (U.S. Department of Health, Education, and Welfare 1975). However, according to both parents and children in this survey, the majority of the target children had visited a dentist in 1976 or 1977. This was less likely for index than comparison children (59 versus 64 percent, according to parents). The only statistically significant difference on these variables was that fewer index than comparison children reported going to a dentist in 1976-77 (53 versus 63 percent; $\chi^2 = 11$, df = 4, p = .05).

CHILDREN'S PROBLEMS AND UTILIZATION OF OTHER SERVICES

The parents and target children were asked about other behaviors and problems of the children that might require some type of service.

Some questions centered around use of drugs, alcohol, and cigarettes and problems with legal authorities. Other items focused on the provision of or need for mental health services, child abuse and child neglect services, delinquency services, and, for youngsters aged 14 to 17, drug and alcohol abuse services. For each of these services, parents were asked specifically if the target child had received them during 1976. Community agencies that provided these services in each site were sent a list of the target children's names and asked to check their 1976 case-load records and return to the research team the number of children in each of two (unnamed) groups who were in their 1976 case load. This "community validation survey" is discussed in greater detail in Chapter 1.

Target Children Receiving Mental Health Services

Table 3.12 indicates the percentage of target children reported by parents and the eight-to-seventeen-year-old respondents as having received mental health services at various times. Based on the parents' responses, it does not appear that the numbers are terribly large. However, a substantially greater proportion of the children reported that they were currently in treatment, as indicated by the last row in Table 3.12. It cannot be determined with complete

TABLE 3.12

Mental Health Services Received by Eight-to-Seventeen-Year-Old Children (percentages of target children)

When Received	Parents' Response I	Parents' Response C	Child's Response I	Child's Response C	Community Validation I	Community Validation C
In 1976	1	2	n.a.*	n.a.	2	5
Before 1976	3	1	n.a.	n.a.	n.a.	n.a.
Now in treatment	2	0	17	2	n.a.	n.a.

*Not applicable.

Note: Figures are rounded. Calculations in each category/row are based on a total of n = 126 in each group.

confidence which of the data are more accurate, but the following considerations are particularly relevant.

The question for both parents and children specifically focused only upon mental health treatment received from a "mental health center," "child guidance center," or "psychiatric clinic." It is possible that some children could have combined counseling received in another setting (for example, at school) with the settings read from the questionnaire. However, there was evidence from the community validation survey that the parents substantially underreported the children's receipt of mental health services. That survey did not encompass all such facilities in each community but did include the major ones. Table 3.12 indicates that the parents underreported by about 50 percent (as compared to reports by community agencies). In view of the incomplete coverage in the community validation survey, it seems reasonable to assume that the parents' underreporting was even greater.

It is of interest to compare these reported data to data from a survey conducted by the National Institute of Mental Health (NIMH). The NIMH reported that only 1 percent of all children aged seven to 17 in the United States were admitted to outpatient psychiatric facilities and community health centers in 1975. (These unpublished data were provided by Carl Taube of the Division of Biometry and Epidemiology, NIMH.) The data are not precisely comparable because the NIMH survey used admissions while our survey focused on whether a child was in treatment in 1976, before 1976, or currently. Moreover, the NIMH survey covered 1975 only. These limitations notwithstanding, on its face, it appears that both index and comparison children are at very high risk compared to the population of all children.

As noted previously, in the subsample covered in the school survey, teachers perceived index children as being in greater need of individual mental health counseling than comparison children. Group differences (46 versus 26 percent) were statistically significant ($\chi^2 = 3.4$, df = 1, $p < .05$).

It should be noted that only three of the parent respondents indicated ever having received family counseling as part of the child's treatment. All were in the index group.

Child Abuse and Neglect

Table 3.13 depicts the percentage of parent respondents who indicated that the target child had been a victim of abuse or neglect. In terms of abuse or neglect "ever" occurring, the index parents were substantially more likely than comparison parents to answer in the affirmative. (Although the numbers are small, it should be noted

TABLE 3.13

Abuse and Neglect Inflicted on Eight-to-Seventeen-Year-Old Children (in percentages)

Occurrences of Abuse/Neglect	Parents' Response I	Parents' Response C	Community Validation I	Community Validation C
Child abuse ever occurred	13	3	n.a.[a]	n.a.
Child neglect ever occurred	19	4	n.a.	n.a.
Child abuse or neglect recorded in 1976[b]	2	2	9–14[c]	11–14[c]

[a]Not applicable.

[b]Recorded by the court, police, or social service agency.

[c]The lower percentage assumes that the courts, police, and social service agencies received reports on the same children. The higher percentage assumes that these organizations received reports on different children.

that the school survey results showed that teachers were 3.5 times more likely to indicate that index children required protective services than comparison children. They indicated that 15 percent of index children [7 out of 46] and 4 percent of comparison children required this service. When "don't know" answers are excluded, the percentages are 28 percent [seven of 29] and 6 percent [two of 34] of index and comparison children, respectively.)

Underreporting is believed to be a substantial problem in interpreting data on these types of socially unacceptable behaviors. The results of the community validation survey, also shown in Table 3.13, suggest that index parents reported a maximum of only about 14 to 22 percent (two out of 14 and two out of nine, respectively) of the cases recorded by the courts, police, or social service agencies and comparison parents a maximum of only about 14 to 18 percent (two out of 14 and two out of 11, respectively). Further, because the community validation survey represents responses received from only 80 percent of police departments, 60 percent of the courts, 80 percent of the public child protective service agencies, and 76 percent of other social service agencies, the actual number of recorded cases of abuse and neglect was undoubtedly higher than these data indicate. And it is believed that a rather small fraction of actual incidents of abuse and neglect are ever actually recorded nationwide. It can only be concluded that a sizable proportion of these children have been victims of abuse or neglect.

It would be desirable to interpret these data in light of comparable data on incidence or prevalence of abuse or neglect in other populations. Unfortunately, such data are scant and of questionable validity (Webb et al. 1975). The only national study conducted using state reporting systems computed an annual rate for abuse of 8.4 per 100,000 children (Gil 1968; Gil 1969). Saad Nagi (1975) estimated the number of reported cases of abuse and neglect in the United States by using a probability sample of official agencies. Thus, his sources were comparable to those used in our community validation survey. This resulted in an estimated annual rate of 8.8 cases per 100,000.

Whatever the shortcomings of these other data, it is nevertheless interesting to note that this survey found rates of recorded abuse or neglect in the index group <u>at least</u> 10.2 to 15.9 times higher than the rates of recorded abuse or neglect reported by Nagi for the United States. (Converting our percents to rates per 100,000 yields 90 per 100,000 to 140 per 100,000 for the index group, compared to Nagi's 8.8 per 100,000. Rates for the comparison group were 110 per 100,000 to 140 per 100,000.) These differences could be partially attributable to differences in reporting laws among the states and other factors. However, it is unlikely that combined effects of these factors could account for a very large proportion of the difference. And the conclusion would still be unambiguous: <u>these children are at very high risk of abuse and neglect</u>.

Delinquency

Table 3.14 indicates that 18 percent of both index and comparison children 11 to 17 years old reported having been "in trouble with the police" at some time. However, index children reported substantially more encounters than did comparison children ($\bar{X}$ = 2.3 and 1.3, respectively) and were considerably more likely to be accused of more serious offenses. Parents reported very similar data. Seven index and two comparison youngsters reported being held in detention or by police at least once.

According to parent respondents (see Table 3.15), index children were considerably more likely than comparison children to have been picked up by police and (although the numbers are small) more likely to have appeared in juvenile court, found to be delinquent, and placed on probation.

TABLE 3.14

Problems with Police As Reported by 11 to 17 Year Olds

	Index	Comparison
Ever been in trouble with with the police (percentage)		
Yes	18	18
No	75	80
Don't know/no response	7	2
Total	100	100
Mean number of times	2.3	1.3
Reason for problem (number)		
Stealing or robbery	6	1
Hurting someone	2	1
Skipping school	1	1
Drugs	1	0
Alcohol	0	0
Traffic violation	1	1
Other	5	8
Total	16	12

Note: Figures are rounded. Percentage calculations are based on 67 index and 66 comparison children.

It is concluded that index children appeared to be more at risk than comparison children of committing delinquent acts and that the acts committed were likely to be of a more serious nature. The cell frequencies were too small to permit statistical testing of these group differences.

Data from the community validation survey were incomplete. They did indicate that four comparison youngsters and one index youngster were listed as delinquent and/or on probation during 1976. Parents' reports indicated that there were four index children and one comparison child involved with the court in 1976 for delinquent acts. The same number (and probably some of the same youngsters) were reportedly on probation in 1976. The data suggest that comparison parents underreported their children's involvement with legal authorities in 1976.

TABLE 3.15

Encounters of Eight to Seventeen Year Olds with the Criminal Justice System: Parents' Responses (in percentages)

Encounter	1976 I	1976 C	Before 1976 I	Before 1976 C
Picked up by police	n.a.	n.a.	10	2
Child appeared in juvenile court for delinquency	3	1	5	2
Found to be delinquent	n.a.	n.a.	2	0
On probation	3	1	n.a.	n.a.

n.a. = Not applicable.

Note: Figures are rounded. Calculations in each category are based on a total of n = 126.

It was noted previously that index children were more likely than comparison children to answer "true" to the statement "I get into a lot of fights" (19 versus 10 percent). They were also significantly less likely (46 versus 63 percent) to answer "true" to the statement "Policemen are well thought of in my family" ($\chi^2 = 7.2$, df = 1, $p < .01$).

Use of Drugs by Target Children

Table 3.16 indicates that 8 percent of the index children and 4 percent of the comparison children admitted to using drugs without a prescription. This difference was not statistically significant. Nearly all of these children stated that marijuana was the only drug they had ever tried. Five of these index children and no comparison children answered "yes" to the question "Have you ever had any bad 'trips' or felt bad after taking drugs?" Two of these children indicated more than two such bad experiences.

Parents of the 16 index and 22 comparison youngsters, aged 14 to 17, stated that three (19 percent) of these index youngsters (and no comparison youngsters) had received drug treatment during 1976. The community validation data indicated that five (31 percent)

TABLE 3.16

Use of Drugs by Eight-to-Seventeen-Year-Old Children (in percentages)

Drug Use	Index	Comparison
Ever tried marijuana or or other drugs		
Yes	8	4
No	89	95
Don't know/refused	3	1
Total	100	100

Note: Figures are rounded and based on n = 126 for both index and comparison children.

of the 16 index teenagers and three (14 percent) of the 22 comparison teenagers were enrolled in drug treatment programs in 1976.

In view of the very small numbers, no firm conclusions can be drawn. However, it is interesting to note that the pattern is the same as for other variables. Index children were more likely to be abusing drugs and in drug treatment programs.

Use of Alcohol

Table 3.17 depicts the frequency of alcohol use reported by the target children. Approximately the same number of child respondents in each group indicated that they had used alcohol at some time, but a higher proportion of index children responding indicated that they drank "once or twice a week." Similarly, a slightly higher proportion of index children stated that they drink "now." No statistical tests of significance were performed because of the small cell frequencies.

Parent respondents were asked questions similar to those asked of their children. Their answers were remarkably similar, although parents were slightly more likely to indicate that the target children used alcohol. Parent respondents did not indicate that any of the children aged 14 to 17 were in alcohol treatment in 1976. (Two index and two comparison parents responded "don't know" to the question of alcohol treatment.) However, the agencies participating in the survey reported that six (37 percent) of the 16 index youngsters aged 14 to 17

TABLE 3.17

Alcohol Use by Eight-to-Seventeen-Year-Old Children (in percentages)

Drinking	Index	Comparison
Frequency of use (by children who ever used)		
Tried a few times	65	85
Once or twice a week	21	11
More than once or twice a week	0	0
Don't know/no response	14	4
Total	100	100
Drinks now		
Yes	9	5
No	91	95
Total	100	100

Note: Figures are rounded. Calculations for frequency of use are based on 29 index and 27 comparison children. Those for the category "drinks now" are based on 11 index and 6 comparison children.

were in alcohol treatment programs. There was no report of any of the 22 comparison youngsters being in alcohol treatment.

No firm conclusions can be drawn because of the small numbers involved. However, again the pattern is the same as for other variables. Index children appeared to be more at risk than comparison children.

Use of Cigarettes

Compared to 17 percent of the comparison children, 23 percent of index target children stated that they had ever smoked cigarettes. Table 3.18 indicates that comparison children were likely to indicate heavier smoking and were slightly more likely to be current smokers.

There are no data on smoking among children in the United States that are completely comparable to these data. However, it is nevertheless interesting to note that a recent survey of teenage

TABLE 3.18

Cigarette Smoking by Eight-to-Seventeen-Year-Old Children (in percentages)

Smoking	Index	Comparison
Frequency of smoking (by children who ever smoked)		
Tried only a few times	66	48
Less than one a day	7	10
1-11 a day	24	33
> 11 a day	0	10
Don't know	3	0
Total	100	101
Smokes now		
Yes	6	8
No	94	92
Total	100	100

Note: Figures are rounded. Calculations for frequency of smoking are based on 29 index and 21 comparison children. Those for the category "smokes now" are based on n = 126 for both index and comparison children.

smoking (U.S. Public Health Service 1976), conducted in 1974, concluded that 15.8 percent of boys aged 12 to 18 and 15.3 percent of girls aged 12 to 18 were "current regular smokers" (that is, smoked "one or more cigarettes per week or one or more per day"). In contrast, 6 percent of the index and 8 percent of the comparison child respondents indicated that they currently "smoked cigarettes" (though they were not asked how frequently they smoked). It is hazardous to draw very much from such noncomparable data, but it would appear that both index and comparison children were less likely to be current smokers than children in their approximate age group in the general U.S. population.

Running Away from Home

The official definition of a runaway child is one who is away from home overnight without permission. Eight index (6 percent) and four comparison (3 percent) parents stated that the target child in their family had run away at least once by this definition. Low cell frequencies prohibit statistical testing of these differences. The mean number of runaway episodes was 2.2 for index children and 2.4 for comparison children who were runaways. No comparable data are available for other populations on running away from home. (Data from the National Statistical Survey on Runaway Youth were carefully examined but were found not to be comparable to our own data.)

Again, the pattern of index children being more at risk than comparison children is maintained, although the numbers are too small to permit drawing firm conclusions on this variable by itself.

INDEX PARENTS AND DRUG TREATMENT

Reports of Parent Respondents

Data collected from index parent respondents indicated that 28 (22 percent) of the respondents were involved in family counseling (or family therapy) at their drug treatment program. Approximately two-thirds of these respondents felt that including other members of their family in counseling sessions was "very helpful." Most of the remaining respondents felt that this practice was "somewhat helpful" to "a little helpful." Of these 28 respondents, 57 percent reported that their spouse or partner was involved in the counseling session, and approximately one-third reported that their children and "other" adults were included in sessions.

When asked what services their drug treatment program could provide that would be helpful to their children and families, 22 percent of the 126 respondents replied "none," 11 percent either replied "don't know" or refused to answer, and 67 percent provided the list of services presented in Table 3.19. As shown, 23 percent of these 84 parents would like recreational services for themselves and their children. Several other services desired by small percentages of these clients involved their children directly, for example, counseling and psychiatric care for their children, family counseling sessions that include the children, and medical care and drug education for children.

Reports of Staff of Drug Treatment Programs: Sites 4-5

The majority of clients at Sites 2-5 consented to a questionnaire being sent to their drug treatment program to gather information on them, their family, and the treatment provided. Questionnaires were

TABLE 3.19

Services Index Parents Believe Would Help Their Children and Families: Sites 2-5

Type of Service	Percentage Responding
Recreational activities for parents/children	23
Help clients find employment	15
Counseling sessions with other family members (parents, children, relatives)	14
Counseling/psychiatric care for children	12
Medical care for clients and family	11
Educate children about drugs	11
Financial help	11
More understanding counselors	9
Counseling/psychiatric care for parents	9
Cut restrictions on attending counseling sessions	8
Better rehabilitation services	8
Establish ways to keep clients' drug problems confidential	8
Vocational training	7
Help find better housing	2

Note: Figures are rounded and based on a total of n = 84.

returned by program staff only from Sites 4 and 5. All 28 forms on consenting clients were returned from Site 4; 21 of 27 forms on consenting clients were returned from Site 5.

Table 3.20 shows the length of time clients at Sites 4-5 had been enrolled in their current programs and in other drug treatment programs before their enrollment in their present settings. In Site 4, the majority of clients had been enrolled in their present programs for one to two years. In Site 5, the majority had been enrolled for either one to two years or for more than five years. These are unusually long periods of treatment when compared to data reported from other sources (see, for example, Burt, Glynn, and Sowder 1979). This finding raises the question as to whether parenthood stabilizes the addicts' life to a great extent and encourages them to stay in treatment. Data collected in this study cannot provide an answer to

TABLE 3.20

Length of Parents' Enrollment in Drug Treatment Programs: Sites 4-5 (in percentages)

Length of Enrollment	Current Program Site 4	Current Program Site 5	Prior Program Site 4	Prior Program Site 5
< 1 year	11	19	0	00
1-2 years	64	33	29	17
3-5 years	25	9	0	33
> 5 years	0	29	0	0
Don't know	0	9	71	50
Total	100	99	100	100

Note: Figures are rounded. Calculations for the current program are based on n = 28 for Site 4 and n = 21 for Site 5. Those for the prior program are based on n = 7 and n = 6 for Sites 4 and 5, respectively.

TABLE 3.21

Types of Treatment Provided Parents by Drug Treatment Programs: Sites 4-5 (in percentages)

Type of Treatment	Site 4	Site 5	Total
Methadone maintenance	100	95	98
Methadone detoxification	71	19	49
Detoxification	7	14	10
Outpatient drug free	18	5	12
Therapeutic community	7	5	6
Day treatment	18	10	14

Note: Figures are rounded and based on n = 28 for Site 4 and n = 21 for Site 5.

this question, but they do suggest that this may be an issue for further research.

As shown, staff often did not know how long the clients were enrolled in other programs before coming to their present program.

Table 3.21 shows the percentage of these clients who received different types of treatment at their present programs. All but one client at these programs had been in a methadone maintenance modality since enrollment in the program. Other types of services provided varied by program. This was especially true for methadone detoxification, which was provided to 71 percent of the Site 4 clients, but to only 19 percent of the Site 5 clients, sometime during their treatment process.

In Site 4, no effort had been made by program staff to contact members of clients' families in three (11 percent) of the cases. In the majority (71 percent) of the remaining cases, five or more efforts had been made to contact clients' families. In Site 5, no effort had been made to contact one-third of the clients' families. In approximately 50 percent of the remaining cases, at least three attempts had been made to contact members of clients' families. Personal contacts by program staff were more likely to have been made with family members than contacts by telephone in both sites. Contacts with the clients' spouses were most likely to have been made when the clients entered treatment and several months after treatment. The few contacts with children and other family members were most likely to have been made several months after the clients' entry into treatment. Contacts at some period in time with some family members were reported in 89 percent of the cases in Site 4 and in 62 percent of the cases in Site 5.

Table 3.22 shows the various ways in which family members were involved in the clients' treatment. These mainly included social activities at the program, assisting staff in setting goals for the clients, participation in family counseling, and/or enrollment of the spouses in drug treatment. In 20 percent of the total cases, families of the clients reportedly had not been involved in any way in the drug treatment of the clients.

In Site 4, six clients had received family counseling for less than one year at the time of survey, and four had received this service for more than one year. Thus, ten (36 percent) of Site 4 clients reportedly received family counseling according to staff (although 13 clients reported receiving this treatment). In Site 5, six clients had received family counseling for less than a year and five for more than a year. Altogether, 48 percent of this subsample of Site 5 clients reportedly had received family counseling (although only eight clients commented on this treatment). The majority (82 percent) of these clients had received an average of one to three hours of family

TABLE 3.22

Ways in Which Family Members Are Involved in the Parents' Drug Treatment: Sites 4-5
(in percentages)

Involvement	Site 4	Site 5	Total
In social activities	57	19	41
In setting goals for client	32	43	37
In family counseling	32	33	33
In treatment themselves	39	19	31
In helping in crisis	0	14	6
In parenting program	7	0	4
Not involved in any way	14	28	20

Note: Figures are rounded and based on n = 28 for Site 4 and n = 21 for Site 5.

counseling per week from counselors who had had at least one year of training in family counseling (or family therapy).

The data suggest that "spouses" were the family members most involved in the family counseling. This included spouses of all clients who had received family counseling in Site 4 and six spouses of the 11 clients who had received family counseling in Site 5. Four children appeared to have been involved in family counseling in Site 5 and one in Site 4. Clients' parents and other relatives were rarely involved (five cases of this were reported). According to staff reports, three clients in Site 4 and two clients in Site 5 had received family counseling outside the program. One child was involved regularly in this counseling at Site 4.

Table 3.23 shows the goals set by staff of drug treatment programs for these clients, together with the percentage of clients involved in each goal. Helping the clients become drug free was a goal for almost 75 percent of the total clients; helping them stay on methadone maintenance and improve their family relationships were goals for nearly two-thirds of the total clients; and helping with jobs/education, emotional problems, and parental functioning applied to 53 to 58 percent of the total clients.

Staff reported that family members assumed responsibilities in goal setting for the clients in a number of ways. In Site 4, nine clients were helped by family members to stay drug free by such means as

TABLE 3.23

Goals Set by Staff of Drug Programs for Parents: Sites 4-5 (in percentages)

Goal	Site 4	Site 5	Total
Help client become drug free	82	59	73
Help client stay on methadone maintenance	68	59	64
Help improve family relationships	64	59	62
Help client with job and/or educational/training needs	43	82	58
Help client solve emotional problems	57	47	53
Help improve parental functioning	57	47	53

Note: Figures are rounded and based on n = 28 for Site 4 and n = 17 for Site 5. In Site 5, four staff did not respond.

the spouses themselves being in treatment or remaining drug free (three cases); encouragement from their parents, siblings, or children; and financial support. Only two comparable instances were mentioned in Site 5, and these revolved around providing the client emotional support. Family members reportedly tried to help clients stay on methadone in ways similar to those just described for helping clients become drug free. In both sites, family members assisted the clients with their emotional problems by attending therapy or marital counseling (three cases) and/or helping clients communicate and/or control their emotions. In six instances, the spouse or parent had taken steps to help the clients secure employment or training. In seven cases, family members made special efforts to improve family relations by coming to therapy and/or working on family communication problems. In 11 cases, family members were involved in efforts to improve parental functioning. In Site 4, four clients/spouses were involved in a positive parenting program.

In Site 4, children reportedly had not been provided any services by the drug treatment programs in 28 percent of the cases. The corresponding figure for Site 5 was 57 percent. Recreational services were provided the respondent clients' children in 38 percent of the Site 5 families. Four other children were provided four other services (group counseling, day treatment, guidance, and odd jobs around the office). In Site 4, six children were enrolled in a positive parenting

TABLE 3.24

Types of Services Provided Index Parents/Families by Community Agencies through Liaison Arrangements: Sites 4-5
(percentages receiving service)

Type of Service	Adults		Children	
	Site 4	Site 5	Site 4	Site 5
Medical	75	71	12	29
Employment	62	41	0	1
Welfare	87	29	1	1
Help with schooling/ vocational training	50	35	1	35
Help in obtaining better housing	19	12	0	0
Psychiatric services	19	12	1	12
Help with probation/ legal authorities	12	18	0	0
Other*	1	0	1	12

*Included alcohol treatment for one adult and day-care for three children.

Note: Figures are rounded and based on 16 families for Site 4 and 17 families for Site 5.

program, ten children were provided referral services, three received counseling, and one was provided family counseling.

Liaison arrangements with other community agencies had been made to provide services to 16 (57 percent) of the Site 4 clients and 17 (81 percent) of the Site 5 clients. Table 3.24 shows the kinds of services provided adults and children in these clients' families by other community agencies. Adults in these families were most likely to be provided medical services, assistance in obtaining employment, and welfare assistance. Children were most likely to be provided medical services.

However, other clients and families reported upon were likely to be receiving some type of services from community agencies without liaison being provided by drug treatment staff. Table 3.25 shows the types of services provided to adults and children in the clients' families without liaison arrangements. For adults and children,

TABLE 3.25

Types of Services Provided Index Parents/Families by Community Agencies without Liaison Arrangements: Sites 4-5
(percentages receiving service)

	Adults		Children	
Type of Service	Site 4	Site 5	Site 4	Site 5
Medical	21	24	7	0
Employment	18	5	0	0
Welfare	18	9	0	9
Help with schooling/ vocational training	0	0	0	5
Help in obtaining better housing	0	5	0	5
Psychiatric services	0	0	4	5
Help with probational/ legal authorities	0	5	0	0
Day-care/nursery service	0	0	0	9

Note: Figures are rounded and based on 28 families for Site 4 and 21 families for Sitc 5.

these were most likely to be medical, employment, and welfare services.

In summary, many of the clients at Sites 4 and 5 were provided services to help their children and their families.

FACTOR ANALYSIS

A factor analysis was conducted for the purpose of determining the underlying structures of the variables included. The procedure used extracted factors that are orthogonal or uncorrelated and rotated by the Varimax method. Thus, any variable that is not in any of the factors is uncorrelated with all five resultant factors. Any variable that loaded on different factors represents a complex variable consisting of different dimensions that are uncorrelated with each other.

The following variables were included in the factor analysis:

- Sex of child
- Child's birthweight
- Unusual conditions at birth
- Current health status of the child
- Number of emergency room visits by child in 1976
- Number of visits by child to doctor for illness in 1976
- Child victim of abuse at any time
- Child victim of neglect at any time
- Child picked up by police before 1976
- Mother used heroin while pregnant with target child
- Mother used other drugs while pregnant with target child
- Number of hours parent does things with child
- Grandparents help raise child
- Sources of financial support for children
- Age of parent
- Race of parent
- Family income
- Parent's employment status
- Parent's years of schooling
- Parent's arrest record
- Parent lives with legal spouse/unmarried partner
- Parent lives alone
- Policemen are well-thought-of by family
- Hug and kiss a lot in family
- Family members often stay up late at night
- Family visits friends or relatives together
- Child gets into a lot of fights
- Child thinks good luck is more important than hard work
- Child believes "When I get into trouble it is my own fault"
- Received help from mental health center
- Ever received tutoring in school
- Ever received counseling in school

The factors described below had eigenvalues of 0.958 or greater (factor loadings are indicated in parentheses).

Family Characteristics

The factor of family characteristics is composed of being black (0.48), having a low family income (-0.55), being unemployed (-0.42), not living with spouse (-0.69), and living alone (0.63). No variables addressing the child are in this factor.

Child's Health

Poorer health status of the child (0.52), number of emergency room visits in 1976 (0.66), number of visits to the doctor in 1976 (0.61), and victim of neglect at any time (0.43) compose the factor of child's health. There is no sizable loading on "child abuse at any time" (0.19). The factor loading for child abuse and neglect should be viewed with caution in view of the considerable underreporting discussed earlier in this chapter.

External Support

The factor of external support consists of the child's grandparents helping to raise the child (0.46), the child's grandparents or other relatives providing financial support for the child (0.45), the child being at any time a victim of abuse (0.38) or neglect (0.34), and the child having never received tutoring in school (-0.35).

Drug Use During Pregnancy

The factor of drug use during pregnancy is composed only of heroin use during pregnancy (0.55), other drug use during pregnancy (0.46), and greater age of parent (0.57). Admitted drug use during pregnancy did not correlate substantially with any other variables.

Sex/Fighting

Factor loadings for sex/fighting were on sex of child (male) and child getting into a lot of fights (-0.41 and 0.39, respectively). There was a minor loading on heroin use by the mother during pregnancy (0.30).

Conclusions

Few variables entered the factors, and the loadings of those that did enter were not particularly high. The results are reassuring in that they suggest that the differences in demographic characteristics between the index and comparison groups do not bias the results. It was noted early in this chapter that the index and comparison groups were significantly different in respondent's sex, age, marital status, spouse's employment, and family income. Of these variables, only family income and marital status (that is, "not living with spouse" and "living alone") entered any of the factors. These entered only the first factor. That factor suggests the rather obvious conclusion that lower family income is associated with being black, unemployed, and living alone (and therefore not having two incomes).

Of additional interest is that the drug use items did not have any other items load on their factor, thus indicating a surprising lack of correlation.

The results of a factor analysis conducted for the comparison group show very similar results.

4
CONCLUSIONS AND IMPLICATIONS

CONCLUSIONS

The basic research question, posed in Chapter 1, was, Are the children of heroin addicts at greater risk than other children for health, learning, behavioral, socioemotional, and/or adjustment problems?

This basic research question consists, of course, of several questions. For example, are the children of heroin addicts at greater risk for health problems than other children? Are they at greater risk for learning problems? For behavioral problems?

Answers to these various questions require further research, given the limitations of this study (see Table A.6 in the Appendix). However, based on this study's findings, children of addicts appear to be at greater risk, or possibly at greater risk, than other children in only some of the above problem areas. In other areas, both the addicts' (index) children and their comparison peers appear to be at high risk when compared to children in the general population.

Index Children at Greater Risk

Table 4.1 summarizes the data on two areas in which the index group seemed clearly at greater risk than the comparison group: learning and/or school adjustment problems and delinquency/behavioral problems. Although all the data shown could not be tested statistically because of small sample sizes, the findings are consistent with statistically significant ones, and the data presented represent multiple data sources.

TABLE 4.1

Problem Areas in Which Index Children Are at "Greater Risk" Than Comparison Children

Problem Area	Data Source
Learning problems and/or school adjustment problems	
Poor performance on IQ and perceptual-motor tests[a]	Test performance of 3-7 year olds
More behavioral problems in classroom[a]	Teachers' reports on subsample of 8-17 year olds
More likely to have "ever" received tutoring[a]	Reports of 8-17 year olds
Parent more likely to be contacted by school for child's misbehavior[a]	Parents of 8-17 year olds
Parent more likely to be contacted by school for child's misbehavior[b]	Site 1 parents
More school failures[a]	Teachers' reports on subsample of 8-17 year olds
More likely to miss six or more days of school[a]	Teachers' reports on subsample of 8-17 year olds
More likely to skip school or be told not to come by school staff[b]	Reports of Site 1 and Sites 2-5 parents
Parent more likely to be contacted by school because of child's absences[b]	Reports of Site 1 and Sites 2-5 parents
Delinquency/behavioral problems	
Child more likely to appear before juvenile court and/or be found delinquent before 1976[b]	Reports of parents of 8-17 year olds

(continued)

TABLE 4.1 (continued)

Problem Area	Data Source
More encounters with police and for more serious offenses[b]	Reports of 11-17 year olds, parents of 8-17 year olds
Children more likely to do work for "pay" that would get them "in trouble with the police"[b]	Reports of 8-17 year olds
Children more likely to get into "a lot of fights"[c]	Reports of 8-17 year olds
More likely to receive counseling in school for "fighting"[b]	Reports of 8-17 year olds
More destructive of school property[b]	Teachers' reports on subsample of 8-17 year olds
More likely to be "runaways"[b]	Reports of Site 1 and Sites 2-5 parents
More likely to use drugs and/or alcohol[b]	Reports of 8-17-year-old children and their parents
More likely to have received drug and/or alcohol treatment in 1976[b]	Community validation forms on 14-17 year olds

[a]Statistically significant at .05.

[b]Could not be tested because of small cell frequencies but consistent with statistically significant results in same problem area.

[c]Not statistically significant but consistent with other trends.

TABLE 4.2

Problem Areas in Which Index Children Are at "Possible Greater Risk" than Comparison Children

Problem Area	Data Source
Mental health/socioemotional problems	
Higher utilization of mental health services before 1976 and during 1976[a]	Parents' reports and community agency reports on 8-17 year olds
Greater perceived need for individual mental health counseling[b]	Teachers' reports on subsample of 8-17 year olds
Greater perceived need for family counseling[c]	Teachers' reports on subsample of 8-17 year olds
More likely to have received school counseling[c]	Reports of 8-17 year olds
More likely to be currently receiving mental health services[a]	Reports of 8-17 year olds
More likely to be judged to have "severe-moderate" socioemotional problems[b]	Blind ratings of three clinicians of 3-7 year olds' figure drawings
Health problems	
More likely to have parents rate current health as only "fair-poor"[b]	Site 1 and Sites 2-5 parents' reports
More likely to rate own current health as only "fair-poor"[b]	Reports of 8-17-year-old children

[a]Could not be tested because of small cell frequencies but consistent with statistically significant results in same problem area.

[b]Statistically significant at .05.

[c]Not statistically significant but consistent with other trends.

Index Children "Possibly at Greater Risk"

Table 4.2 shows two areas in which the index children are "possibly at greater risk" than comparison children. One is mental health and/or socioemotional problems. In this regard, some findings shown in the table are not statistically significant, although the results shown are consistent with other trends.

In summary, the findings on mental health/socioemotional problems are not as clear as those for learning/school adjustment problems. Hence, the term "possibly at greater risk." Further, compared with national figures, both groups appeared to be at risk when judged by their utilization of mental health services in 1976.

Considerably less convincing are the findings on health problems. As shown in Table 4.2, index parents and the eight-to-seventeen-year-old children were significantly more likely than their comparison counterparts to perceive the target child's current health as only "fair-poor" (according to self-reports).

However, other findings suggest that there were no greater health problems (current or at birth) among the eight-to-seventeen-year-old index children than there were among their comparison peers. Among the three-to-seven-year-old index group, however, there were higher rates of low birthweight, a greater need for medical attention at birth, and a greater utilization of emergency room services in 1976 than among the three-to-seven-year-old comparison children, though these differences were either not statistically significant or could not be tested because of low expected cell frequencies. Thus, the question of whether or not the index children are at greater risk for health problems cannot be answered conclusively. The data merely suggest somewhat greater health risks among the index group.

Both Groups at Risk

Data collected from community agencies suggest that both the index and comparison children are at especially high risk for abuse and neglect. The rates for abuse and neglect among children in this study were 10.2 to 15.9 times higher than rates calculated by Nagi (1975) from official records nationwide. Index parents' reports on abuse and neglect of their children before 1976 add confirmation to the community survey findings. Further, as noted previously, it is highly probable that the rates of abuse and neglect among these study populations were underreported by all data sources.

Also, as noted previously, both groups appear to be at risk for mental health problems.

DISCUSSION

The findings suggest that cognitive and social enrichment programs are needed for many of the three-to-seven-year-old children tested at Site 1. However, care should be taken in generalizing the Site 1 findings to other three-to-seven-year-old children of addicts. The sample was small, limited to one site, and perhaps unrepresentative. Certainly the data on the eight-to-seventeen-year-old index children did not suggest such a high incidence of cognitive and/or socioemotional problems as was found among the Site 1 index children (though the sources of data from Sites 2-5 and Site 1 are not totally comparable). School adjustment and/or academic problems among the eight-to-seventeen-year-old index group were seemingly greater than among their comparison peers, but the numbers of children in these different problem categories were generally small. Similarly, the numbers of eight-to-seventeen-year-old index children reported as delinquent and/or having other behavioral problems were small. Abuse and/or neglect rates did appear high, compared to national figures, but they were similar for both the index and comparison groups, according to community validation data. In summary, one should not conclude from these data that surrogate care (for example, coster care) would be either a better or worse alternative for children of addicts.

With proper intervention, the types of problems noted among these children could be mitigated. The index families studied appear to have a number of strengths that could be drawn upon in any intervention process. These parents have high hopes and expectations for their children's future. Education, in particular, seems to be valued by these parents and their children. Assisting parents in enhancing their children's educational achievement (for example, linking them with tutoring services) may be one means of involving these families in intervention and enhancing the development of their children.

Moreover, the eight-to-seventeen-year-old index children and their siblings appeared, in general, to have positive self-images and positive perceptions of their interactions with their families. Interventions designed to capitalize on these strengths might also keep parents and children highly involved in different intervention programs designed to enhance child development outcomes and/or family functioning. Additional suggestions for intervention are presented below.

IMPLICATIONS FOR RESEARCH

Based on the findings of this study, a number of recommendations can be made. First, it is recommended that a similar study be conducted in which developmental testing is done on large samples of addicts' children in different areas of the country. This testing should include older children (eight to 17) as well as younger children (three to seven). Since there are existing norms for these tests, it is not particularly necessary that this testing include a comparison group composed of children of nonaddicts.

Second, a large-scale study should be conducted to obtain additional data on school, health, mental health, abuse/neglect, delinquency, alcohol, and drug problems among children of heroin addicts. Such a study should provide for a longer research time frame than this current study in order that investigators may have time to *carefully* "validate" parent and child responses through contacts with schools and relevant community agencies.

Third, a study should be conducted to determine whether the developmental status of children of addicts is better, the same, or worse when these children are placed in surrogate care than when they are maintained by their addict parents, as well as the conditions under which surrogate care may make some difference (positive or negative).

Finally, NIDA should fund pilot projects with both research and treatment components to determine the impact of providing coordinated, comprehensive services, both directly and through referral networks, to children of addicts who are maintained in the care of their addict parents (see below).

All of the above recommended research strategies, of course, should be based on sound methodologies, including adequate sample sizes and, where appropriate, carefully selected comparison groups. The drawing of equivalent comparison groups, however, may prove difficult, if not impossible, within the time and cost constraints of most research studies. Addicts appear to have unique "life-styles" (in some respects) that may prohibit true equivalency between addict parent groups and any type of nonaddict parent group. The problem of selecting the *most* relevant dimensions on which to match addict and nonaddict parent groups should be, perhaps, the first issue addressed in any research recommended above in which comparison groups will be used.

IMPLICATIONS FOR POLICY

Services Provided by Drug Treatment Programs

The results of this study show clearly that children of addicts are at risk in a number of ways. Many of the problems encountered by these children are amenable to intervention by using appropriate

of these pilot projects be based on the "ideal" model of a comprehensive community mental health center, that is, a service that provides for the "total" needs of the client (including the client's family needs). These various projects should include research components (using pre- and postmeasures where possible) as well as treatment components in order to assess the effectiveness and efficiency of each "model" used. More specific recommendations related to research and development (R&D) projects for different developmental stages of childhood and different childhood problems are discussed below.

The recommendations reflect the findings of the literature review for this project (Sowder 1977) as well as the findings of the survey presented in this study. Therefore, they begin with proposals for R&D projects at the prenatal stage.

Prenatal and Neonatal Considerations

Studies suggest that mortality and morbidity risks to the mother, fetus, and neonate are increased under several conditions that typify the lives of women who are addicted to opiates before, during, and/or after pregnancy (Dickey in press). These conditions include drug addiction, alcohol abuse, poor nutrition and lack of medical care during pregnancy, low socioeconomic status, and poor physical and mental health. No doubt, it will be many years before researchers can clarify just how and why each of these conditions adversely affects prenatal and neonatal outcomes and the extent to which drug ingestion per se contributes to the prenatal and neonatal risks noted among pregnant addicts and their offspring. Until a better understanding is gained, researchers and treatment personnel could work together in an attempt to assist parents and their offspring. They might work toward testing the following hypotheses in a coordinated research and treatment environment.

The first hypothesis maintains that prenatal risks will be higher when women ingest heroin and other drugs (including alcohol) during pregnancy than when (1) they do not or (2) when addicted women are maintained on low dosages of methadone as opposed to no methadone and (1) and (2) are studied comparing groups matched by such factors as age, ethnicity, socioeconomic status, physical/mental health status (including nutritional status), type and extent of drug use during pregnancy, and receipt of and involvement in medical, prenatal, and social-psychological services (including family therapy).

The second hypothesis maintains that, among matched groups (see the first hypothesis), prenatal and neonatal risk rates will be significantly associated with the extent to which each group received comprehensive services that included pre- and postnatal care and medical, social, psychological, employment, and legal services before, during, and after pregnancy (though correlations between increases in services and outcomes may be lower in high-risk than in low-risk groups, for example, groups in the lower socioeconomic strata as opposed to those in higher social classes). The work of Loretta Finnegan and her associates and that of Richard Brotman and his associates substantiates the hypothesis that comprehensive care will enhance mother-infant outcomes (see Dickey in press).

Carefully designed research efforts are needed to determine under which conditions risks increase for the mother, fetus, and/or neonate; under which service-delivery mode risks decrease for the mother, fetus, and/or neonate; the time at which a particular intervention appears most effective in reducing a particular type of risk; and which combination of services proves most effective for different populations of addicted women and their offspring.

NIDA might fund a number of pilot projects that provide comprehensive services to pregnant addicts and their babies and that also have built-in research components. If funds permit, some of these projects could be introduced on a "planned variation" basis; that is, across projects, services could be varied to include different combinations of and emphases on medical, social, psychological, and nutritional services; use of different methods of outreach; direct versus indirect modes of delivery; and so forth. Planning efforts for any type of treatment/service program would need to include sampling considerations so that adequate sample sizes would be available for comparisons of different services' emphases.

One consideration in treatment should be intervention that would strengthen the mother-infant bonding process. Such service components might include live-in hospital arrangements to permit extended contact between the mother and infant, parent education and skills training, and mother-infant contact at birth.

Infancy and Early Childhood

Several studies suggest that infancy and early childhood may be periods in which some children of addicts experience a series of surrogate parents, abuse and neglect, lack of cognitive and social stimulation, developmental deficiencies (in organizational thinking processes and motor and perceptual development), behavioral problems (for example, hyperactivity, temper tantrums), rejection, and inconsistent child-rearing practices (Densen-Gerber and Rohrs 1973; Fanshel 1975; Lodge 1976; Nichtern 1973; Strauss et al. 1976; Wilson et al. 1979; Wilson et al. 1973). The findings of this study support some of the findings in the literature.

The above are problems requiring services that are outside the mandate of most drug treatment programs. If they are to be dealt with by drug treatment staff, services will have to be greatly expanded either by creating new direct services and/or by expanding indirect informal or contractual referral services. Some of the research and treatment efforts might be based on the following hypotheses. First, children of addicts who have experienced early extended contact with their mothers during the neonatal period and whose families continue to be provided comprehensive follow-up services during the child's early formative years will manifest fewer developmental problems than will their peers whose addicted families are not provided these services. Second, children of addicts who are abandoned and/or continually abused or neglected by their parents will show "normal" development if placed for adoption or if they experience stable foster care from early infancy on (provided they are not congenitally handicapped and receive "good" care). Third, the provision of parent education (including infant stimulation techniques) to the addict parents soon after birth and throughout early childhood will enhance the cognitive and social development of these children. And fourth, the provision of early childhood enrichment programs to children of addicts will enhance their cognitive and social development.

The above hypotheses will require a number of carefully designed studies. Ideally, these would include well-matched comparison groups that do not receive the various interventions. The second hypothesis regarding adoption and foster care particularly deserves a good deal of further study since the work of Wilson and her colleagues (1973) suggests that some developmental risks may be due to drug use during pregnancy and not easily overcome by stable caregiving. If these findings are replicated across numerous samples, new intervention strategies will need to be devised for these children and their surrogate caregivers.

Since all research endeavors would need to be tailored to specific populations and interventions, specific designs are not presented here in order to keep the discussion brief.

Service planners might search for communities that have both drug abuse treatment programs and early childhood intervention research and development projects. To drug treatment programs in those communities, NIDA might provide additional monies for services and/or staff trained in child development and parent education. This support would enable drug treatment programs to coordinate efforts with the early childhood programs in order to provide addicted parents and their children the services of these programs (for example, parent education, Head Start services).

Or, NIDA might fund some pilot projects within drug treatment programs that provide parent education and early childhood socialization/educational components as direct services.

The comprehensive services suggested earlier could also be extended to families with preschool-aged children. These would guarantee services for medical, social, and psychological problems that, if untreated, could negate the benefits of educational, social, and cognitive intervention strategies for the children and their parents.

These social services should include protective services. Linkages with protective services/social services agencies that commonly have legal responsibility for child protection pose particularly difficult issues. In some states, children of addicts are presumed to be neglected or abused and therefore can be removed from their parents whether or not parental care is adequate. Further, social work practices vary widely among agencies. Some agencies are considerably more likely to use protective/social services to maintain the children in their own homes than others (Sowder 1977). The importance of this issue cannot be overemphasized in considering programs for addict families. Linkages with protective services/social service agencies may be crucial to the success of programs for addict families. These linkages must be developed with considerable concern for the well-being of the clients.

The suggestions probably would not pertain to children of addicts who are actually placed for adoption and/or foster care. Such children would probably be "lost" to drug treatment programs. However, comprehensive services might well include foster care and adoption services (directly or through referral) and certainly should include strategies that will assist addict parents in making and accepting their decision regarding substitute care for their children and working effectively with caseworkers and foster parents for the benefit of their children.

The School-Aged Child and Adolescent

Although many theorists believe that early childhood experiences lay the basic foundation for human development, the work of Thomas Langner and his colleagues (1974) has shown that developmental outcomes are greatly influenced by experiences during latency age and adolescence.

This survey provides the only data known to the research team on children of addicts past the preschool age (except for two studies on children of addicts in foster care). These survey data suggest high rates of school adjustment problems, delinquency/behavioral problems, abuse and neglect, treatment for substance abuse, and so forth. They suggest also that many addict parents may serve as poor role models in terms of substance-taking behavior and criminal activity. Criminal activity on the part of parents has been shown to be highly related to delinquency among children (Ahlstrom and Havinghurst

1971; California Youth Authority 1973; Glueck and Glueck 1950; Robins and Herjanic 1975).

Early intervention may mitigate some of the above effects, but many children would be too old to benefit from any early intervention efforts that might be established in the near future. Efforts must be planned on the basis of the children's present age and be able to take into account, in many cases, years of continual problems or deprivation of some type. It is, perhaps, this older group that will require the most extensive effort and the greatest degree of mobilization and coordination of a variety of social resources.

The following hypothesis and research and treatment implications are directed toward older children of addicts (ages six to 18) who would not have been recipients of any of the proposed efforts suggested previously, or at least not on any planned basis. Rather, what follows refers to efforts that could be launched in the future for essentially "untreated" older children of addicts.

The hypothesis maintains that older children of addicts who receive a coordinated network of community services, including medical, nutritional, social, psychological, legal, and special education services, when required will, over time, have fewer social, psychological, medical, behavioral, and learning disabilities than will their peers of the same age in addicted families who do not receive these services. (Correlations between positive outcomes and interventions will, no doubt, be higher among groups receiving the intervention at earlier ages and among those with fewer "risk" factors in their lives.)

The above hypothesis contains many complexities that would require carefully designed studies (including well-matched control groups). Ideally, the research would be longitudinal. However, data collected over time by a time series design could provide program planners with useful interim data upon which they could plan resource allocations for future efforts.

NIDA might plan several pilot projects that would enhance the ability of drug treatment programs to build and/or expand their work with families and staffs' ability to mobilize and coordinate community resources in the behalf of children of addicts and their families. Part of this effort might include consultation and training by people in community mental health centers (CMHCs) who are experienced and successful in mobilizing community resources in behalf of problem-ridden families. Research has shown that CMHC personnel have been remarkably successful in such work (Sowder 1974).

The Family

Research suggests that a stable and stimulating familial environment greatly increases the likelihood of positive child development outcomes (Sowder 1977). Many of the above recommendations were focused on strategies that would strengthen family life and parent-child relationships. However, multiproblem families often require extensive support from the human services system that extends beyond the types of services proposed above. Parents, for example, may need the same comprehensive range of services as that required by their children. The discussion here, however, is focused on what appear to be two crucial problem areas, namely, strengthening the parents' ability to provide financially for their children and strengthening family relationships and parenting skills. These problem areas are already being addressed by many drug treatment programs but may, in many programs, need more attention and support. Several hypotheses and research and treatment implications are appropriate for "the family."

The first hypothesis suggests that the upgrading of vocational training and employment services for addict parents will enhance their ability to provide their children adequate nutrition, housing, medical care, and other support necessary for healthy development. Parents in this survey certainly indicated a need for being able to provide better financial support for their children. The second hypothesis maintains that the provision of good family therapy and/or counseling to addict parents and their children will increase family stability and enhance relationships between parents and their children. And the third hypothesis asserts that the provision of parent education programs will enhance the ability of addict parents to effect the positive development of their children.

Carefully designed research studies are needed to determine the kinds of employment or training that would be most beneficial to a particular addict parent population, the type of family therapy/counseling most appropriate for different addict parent populations, and the types of parent education most appropriate for different addict parent populations. The program needs may vary by area and by type of population. For example, if good day-care is unavailable, it may be more advisable to help mothers of young children obtain public assistance than employment while preparing them for future employment when their children are older. Or, different family therapy and parent education interventions may be required for families of different ethnic/racial or social-class backgrounds (for example, white middle-class versus low-income Puerto Rican families). Research should be designed to delineate the services best suited to different types of families.

NIDA might fund a number of research and demonstration projects designed to determine the kinds of employment/training programs and the kinds of family therapy services that would be most effective for different types of addict parent populations. And NIDA might consider providing incentives and/or financial support to all federally funded drug treatment programs in order to enhance existing services or implement new training/employment and family therapy services.

All of the above suggestions imply that drug treatment programs should intervene in the lives of their clients' children and with adult family members other than the client as well as expand their resource capabilities by creating or upgrading their existing family intervention strategies and/or building a coordinated referral network that mobilizes a wide range of community resources. The suggestions imply, moreover, that drug treatment staff will often have to assume an advocate role in behalf of their clients' children and the family as a whole.

The above suggestions also imply that all the proposed treatment efforts should be evaluated in order to plan more effectively for any subsequent intervention.

APPENDIX: TABULAR PRESENTATIONS RELATED TO METHODOLOGY

TABLE A.1

Steps Taken in Sampling the Index Group

1. Screeners contacted each client or every client (depending on the estimated size of the eligible population and/or the populations willing to cooperate) and determined the client's eligibility for the study (that is, whether or not the client maintained responsibility for a child within certain age ranges and had a problem with heroin).

2. Screeners then explained the purpose of the study to the client, the fact that confidentiality would be maintained by the research team, the payment for participating, and the fact that the client would be eligible for the study only if he/she and their child participated together. (Payment was $10 for each target child, $10 for each parent, and $5 for each sibling.)

3. Screeners then asked the client if he/she was willing to participate. If the client was not, the screener attempted to clarify any possible misunderstandings about the study and asked the client again to participate.

4. If the client appeared interested, screeners then obtained permission to interview the client's child (or, in some cases, two children). If permission was not granted, the screener discontinued the screening.

5. If clients consented to their children and themselves being interviewed or tested, the screeners obtained the names and ages of each child in the family. Special respondent selection cards were used to sample one child (or, where required, the target child and a sibling) from each family. This permitted random selection of the children by age group and permitted the team to obtain a balance by age groups.

6. The screener then obtained the name, address, and a phone number for the client.

7. The appointment maker then obtained the completed initial contact form from the screener (as the screener moved on to contact other clients), obtained an identification number (ID) from a master list, placed the ID number on the initial contact form, showed the client the times available for interviewing at a central location (or at home, if necessary), and reiterated some of the study demands to the client.

8. The appointment maker then filled out an appointment reminder form for the client, which included the name(s) of the child(ren)

to be interviewed/tested, the date and time of the appointment for the child/parent, the amount of the incentive for each participant in the family, and a telephone number where the interviewer could be reached if the client had to change the appointment time. The client was also given a brief, written description of the study.

TABLE A.2

Steps Taken in Sampling the Comparison Group

1. The interviewer introduced himself/herself and asked to speak to the male (female) head of the household (that is, the male if they were seeking to match a person with a male index parent and the female head if they were seeking to match to a female index parent).

2. The interviewer explained that a survey was being conducted for HEW, that the person's name was randomly selected from the telephone directory, and that people were being sought who qualified for the study.

3. Promising confidentiality, the interviewer then asked if the person had children living in the household who were within the age range of interest. If not, the interview was discontinued and another participant sought.

4. If the person qualified by having children of the age range under study, the interviewer asked if the children were living at home nine months out of the year and also if there were one or two parents in the household. If the children were not living at home <u>or</u> selection of this respondent entailed exceeding the quota at that site for a one- or two-parent family, the interview was discontinued and another participant sought.

5. If the person remained eligible on all the above, the interviewer then asked whether either parent had been in a drug treatment program since being a parent. If the respondent refused to answer or the answer was "yes," the interviewer asked if either parent used drugs without a prescription since being a parent and, again, discontinued the interview if the response was either a "yes" or a refusal.

6. If the person was still eligible, the interviewer randomly selected one child in the family within the age range of interest, gave a brief explanation of the study and payment incentives to the parent, and scheduled an appointment with the parent and selected children.

TABLE A.3

Sampling Data on Validation Forms by Site
(number of forms)

Type of Information Form	Did Not/Could Not Participate[a]					Provided Usable Data					Total
	Site					Site					
	1	2	3	4	5	1	2	3	4	5	
Mental health	1	5	4	2	5	1	2	1	3	4	28
Abuse/neglect	1	3	3	1	5	4	8	9	10	3	47
Delinquency	n.a.[b]	1	0	1	0	n.a.[b]	0	2	1	1	6
Alcohol abuse (only)	n.a.[b]	4	5	5	3	n.a.[b]	3	4	2	2	35
Drug abuse (only)	n.a.[b]	3	11	4	4	n.a.[b]	2	7	9	2	42
Drug/alcohol abuse	n.a.[b]	1	0	1	2	n.a.[b]	0	3	4	0	11
Total	2	17	23	14	19	5	15	26	36	12	169

[a]Represents both agencies that did not respond at all and those that could not participate for reasons discussed in Chapter 1.

[b]Not applicable. Population too young to warrant mail out of the form.

TABLE A.4

Scoring System for Draw-A-Person and Peabody Vocabulary Tests

Score Range	Classification	
	Draw-A-Person	Peabody Vocabulary
125 and above	Superior	Very rapid learners
110-124	High average (bright)	Rapid learners
90-109	Average	Average learners
75-89	Low average (dull)	Slow learners
Below 75*	Mentally deficient	Very slow learners

*Scored as below tenth percentile in this study.

TABLE A.5

Scoring for Bender-Gestalt for Children Ages Three to Seven (number of errors)

Age	Average Number of Errors for Age	Below Average (Poor) Number of Errors for Age*
3	20.0	> 28
4	17.0	> 22
5	17.0	> 19
6	8.5	> 17
7	6.0	> 9

*Scored as below tenth percentile in this study and based on norms used at the Early Childhood Screening and Prevention Program, Maimonides Community Mental Health Center. The norms were established on a largely multiethnic, low-income population.

TABLE A.6

Limitations of Study: Problems, Possible Consequences, and Solutions

Problem	Possible Consequence	Solution
Randomly selected respondents could refuse to participate.	Self-selection biases of an unknown type could be operating, making the samples unrepresentative of the populations they were supposed to represent.	Two or more contacts were made with potential respondents, when necessary. Every attempt was made to solicit cooperation in order to reduce rates of "volunteerism" (where time permitted).
Geographical representation is limited to five urban sites.	Areas chosen may not be representative of all urban areas.	Programs were selected in geographically dispersed regions to obtain a better cross-sectional sample.
Ethnic representation is limited. Sample selection was focused on Blacks, Anglos, and people of Spanish heritage due to time/cost constraints, which limited interpretation of data to a few cultural/ethnic groups.	American Indians, Asian Americans, and other minority groups are not represented in the findings.	No solution was attempted.

(continued)

TABLE A.6 (continued)

Problem	Possible Consequence	Solution
Child index respondents represent only children living with their parents.	These children may be unrepresentative of children of addicts in surrogate care.	A few questions were asked of parents about the number, ages, sex, and whereabouts of children not living at home and parent-child relationships.
The child sample excludes children under age 3 and above age 17.	Data may not be representative of problems of infants or older children in these families.	The number, ages, and sex of children under 3 were obtained from parents. (It is not possible to interview children under age 3.)
The 3 "matching" criteria for comparison parents could not be used in 100 percent of the cases.	This problem may have introduced some nonequivalence of groups.	Wide Area Telecommunications Service (WATS) interviewers exhausted the potentially eligible respondents in each selected neighborhood. When matching could not be done on 3 criteria, sex of parent respondent was dropped, but age group of child and family structure were retained when possible.
Sample sizes are small in each site.	Rather large differences were necessary for statistical significance. Statistical tests could not be conducted for some variables because of small cell frequencies.	In analysis, categories were collapsed and/or analysis across sites was conducted to increase sample sizes where necessary and appropriate.
Parent/child interview data represent self-reports.	Self-reporting is subject to distortions of memory, response set, acquiescence,	Some "validation" checks were used: asking the parent/child the same questions and analyzing discrepancies and

	and/or a tendency to give socially desirable answers because of a fear of being truthful and/or a desire to please the interviewer.	use of "community validation forms" to check on parents' responses to selected sensitive questions. Also, questionnaire items were checked for internal consistency and given a format that would reduce response set. In addition, only experienced interviewers were used. They were trained to establish easy rapport, assure confidentiality, maintain privacy, etc.
Community validation forms provided only the names of children. Further, there was less than a 100 percent response rate.	Children with common names in this sample could have been misidentified (e.g., a "John Doe" recorded in an agency case load may not have been the "John Doe" in this study) and/or the same child, correctly identified, may have been in the case load of more than one agency. Both could lead to an overestimate of the problem. The less than complete response rate, conversely, could lead to an underestimate of the incidence of a problem.	Because of confidentiality, no identifying information (e.g., an address) accompanied a child's name. Agencies were informed of the age group. Hence, adults with the same name as the children would not have been counted by agencies. Data are reported in ranges, to account for the possibility of more than one agency reporting on the same child. A follow-up letter was sent to enhance the response rate.

(continued)

TABLE A.6 (continued)

Problem	Possible Consequence	Solution
The developmental testing of 3-7 year olds was not done "blindly," i.e., the examiners were aware of the group to which a child belonged.	Some bias may have been introduced (e.g., an expectation of poorer performance among one particular group that influenced the examiner's method of testing.	The clinicians followed standard clinical procedures that are intended to reduce any possible examiner bias. Tests were assessed independently by a clinician not involved in the testing. No biases were found.
The Robbie the Rabbit test was not subjected to validity and reliability checks (due to time/cost constraints) and was used with a very small sample in some sites.	The lack of reliability/validity checks hinders data interpretation as does the small sample size.	Where appropriate, the responses were compared to those of older siblings to check for consistency. Data were combined across sites to increase the sample n.
The screening battery designed to distinguish addicts from nonaddicts was tested on a limited sample (due to time/cost constraints).	The instrument may not have been totally reliable and valid.	A computer analysis was performed on each comparison parent respondent to determine the number of questions he/she responded to in the same way the addicts did on the pretest. Results suggest the instrument distinguishes addicts from nonaddicts. (Other screening questions were used in initial contacts to eliminate persons with drug problems. These rested on self-reports.)

BIBLIOGRAPHY

Ackerman, J. 1976. "Developmental Assessment of All Infants Born to the Family Care Program, 1975-1976." In Symposium on Comprehensive Health Care for Addicted Families and Their Children, edited by R. Brotman and G. Beschner, pp. 99-106. Rockville, Md.: National Institute on Drug Abuse.

Ahlstrom, W. M., and R. G. Havinghurst. 1971. Four Hundred Losers—Delinquent Boys in High School. San Francisco: Jossey-Bass.

Bee, H. 1975. The Developing Child. New York: Harper and Row.

Beine, E. C. 1974. "Social Service Aspects of Drug Addiction in the Newborn." Journal of the National Medical Association 66: 313-27.

Bernstein, B. 1964. "Aspects of Language and Learning in the Genesis of the Social Process." In Language in Culture and Society: A Reader in Linguistics and Anthropology, edited by D. Hymes, pp. 251-63. New York: Harper and Row.

Blinick, G., E. Jerez, and R. C. Wallach. 1973. "Methadone Maintenance, Pregnancy, and Progeny." Journal of the American Medical Association 22: 477-79.

Burt, M. R., T. J. Glynn, and B. J. Sowder. 1979. Psychosocial Characteristics of Drug Abusing Women. Rockville, Md.: National Institute on Drug Abuse.

Burt, M. R., and R. Balyeat. 1976. A Comprehensive Emergency Services System for Neglected and Abused Children. New York: Vantage Press.

California Youth Authority. 1973. A Comparison of Admission Characteristics of Youth Authority Wards, 1962-1971. Sacramento: State of California, Department of Youth Authority.

Chambers, C. D., R. K. Hinesley, and M. Moldestad. 1970. "Narcotic Addiction in Females: A Race Comparison." International Journal of the Addictions 5: 257-78.

Chein, I., D. L. Gerard, R. S. Lee, and E. Rosenfeld. 1964. The Road to H. New York: Basic Books.

Clark, J. S., W. C. Capel, B. M. Goldsmith, and G. T. Stewart. 1972. "Wives, Families, and Junk: A Comparative Study of Heroin Addicts Maintained on Methadone." Journal of Drug Issues 2: 57-65.

Cohn, A. H., F. C. Collingnon, K. Armstrong, L. Barrett, B. DeGraaf, C. Froland, R. Juster, M. K. Miller, and S. S. Ridge. n.d. "Adult Client Working Papers Evaluation. Evaluation, OCD/ SRS Demonstration Program in Child Abuse and Neglect." Xeroxed. Berkeley, Calif.: Berkeley Planning Associates.

Cuskey, W. R., T. Premkumar, and L. Sigel. 1972. "Survey of Opiate Addiction among Females in the United States between 1850 and 1970." Public Health Review 1: 5-39.

DeLeon, G. 1974. "Phoenix House: Psychopathological Signs among Male and Female Drug Free Residents." Addictive Diseases: An International Journal 1: 135-52.

Densen-Gerber, J., and C. C. Rohrs. 1973. "Drug-addicted Parents and Child Abuse." Contemporary Drug Problems: 683-95.

Dickey, S. In press. Pregnancy and Addiction. Rockville, Md.: National Institute on Drug Abuse.

Eldred, C. A., V. V. Grier, and N. Berliner. October 1974. "Comprehensive Treatment for Heroin Addicted Mothers." Social Casework, pp. 470-77.

Ellingwood, E. H., W. G. Smith, and G. E. Vaillant. 1966. "Narcotic Addiction in Males and Females: A Comparison." International Journal of the Addictions 1: 33-45.

Fagan, O., J. C. Gersten, T. S. Langner, and J. Eisenberg. n.d. "Antecedents and Correlates of Illicit Drug Use in a Sample of Urban Youth." Xeroxed. New York: Columbia School of Public Health, Division of Epidemiology. (Cited with permission.)

Fanaroff, A. A., J. H. Kennell, and M. H. Klaus. 1972. "Followup of Low Birthweight Infants—The Predictive Value of Maternal Visiting Patterns." Pediatrics 49: 287-90.

Fanshel, D. 1975. "Parental Failure and Consequences for Children. The Drug-abusing Women Whose Children Are in Foster Care." American Journal of Public Health 65: 604-12.

Freedman, T. G., and L. P. Finnegan. 1976. "Triads and the Drug Dependent Mother." Social Work 21: 400-04.

Gil, D. 1974. "What Schools Can Do About Child Abuse." In The Battered Child: Selected Readings, edited by J. E. Leavitt, pp. 215-20. Morristown, N.J.: General Learning Corporation.

____. 1969. "Physical Abuse of Children: Findings and Implications of a Nationwide Study." Pediatrics 44: 857-64.

____. 1968. "Incidence of Child Abuse and Demographic Characteristics of Persons Involved." In The Battered Child, edited by R. E. Helfer and C. H. Kempe, pp. 19-40. Chicago: University of Chicago Press.

Glueck, S., and E. Glueck. 1950. Unraveling Juvenile Delinquency. New York: Commonwealth Fund.

Harris, D. B. 1963. Children's Drawings as Measures of Intellectual Maturity. New York: Harcourt, Brace, and World.

Johnson, B., and H. A. Morse. 1974. "Injured Children and Their Parents." In The Battered Child: Selected Readings, edited by J. E. Leavitt, pp. 18-23. Morristown, N.J.: General Learning Corporation.

Kadushin, A. 1974. Child Welfare Services. 2nd ed. New York: Macmillan/Collier Macmillan.

Kaplan, D., and R. Reich. 1976. "The Murdered Child and His Killers." American Journal of Psychiatry 133: 809-13.

Klaus, M. H., and J. H. Kennell. 1976. Maternal-Infant Bonding. St. Louis: C. V. Mosby.

Klein, M., and L. Stern. 1971. "Low Birthweight and the Battered Child Syndrome." American Journal of Diseases of Children 122: 15-18.

Koppitz, E. 1971. The Developmental Bender Scoring System for Young Children. New York: Grune and Stratton.

Langner, T. S., J. C. Gersten, E. L. Green, J. Eisenberg, J. Herson, and E. McCarthy. 1974. "Treatment of Psychological Disorders Among Urban Children." Journal of Consulting and Clinical Psychology 42: 170-79.

Langrod, J. 1970. "Secondary Drug Use Among Heroin Users." International Journal of the Addictions 5: 611-35.

Lief, N. 1976. "Some Measures of Parenting Behavior for Addicted and Nonaddicted Mothers." In Symposium on Comprehensive Health Care for Addicted Families and Their Children, edited by R. Brotman and G. Beschner, pp. 38-47. Rockville, Md.: National Institute on Drug Abuse.

Lodge, A. 1976. "Developmental Findings with Infants Born to Mothers on Methadone Maintenance: A Preliminary Report." In Symposium on Comprehensive Health Care for Addicted Families and Their Children, edited by R. Brotman and G. Beschner, pp. 79-85. Rockville, Md.: National Institute on Drug Abuse.

Martin, H. 1972. "The Child and His Development." In Helping the Battered Child, edited by C. H. Kempe and R. E. Helfer, pp. 93-114. Philadelphia: J. B. Lippincott.

Mondanaro, J. 1976. "Pregnancy, Children, and Addiction." In Women in Treatment: Issues and Approaches, edited by A. Bauman, N. Kamar, and M. Tiesan, pp. 61-79. Arlington, Va.: National Drug Abuse Center.

Nagi, S. Z. 1975. "Child Abuse and Neglect Programs: A National Overview." Children Today 4: 13-17.

Nichtern, S. 1973. "The Children of Drug Users." Journal of the American Academy of Child Psychiatry 12: 24-31.

Nurco, D. N., and M. Lerner. 1972. "Characteristics of Drug Users in a Correctional System." Journal of Drug Issues 2: 49-52.

Obitz, F. W., and L. J. Oziel. 1973. "General and Specific Perceived Locus of Control in Delinquent Drug Users." International Journal of the Addictions 8: 723-27.

O'Donnell, J. A. 1969. Narcotic Addicts in Kentucky. Public Health Service Publication no. 1881. Washington, D.C.

Robins, L. N., and B. L. Herjanic. 1975. "Arrests and Delinquency in Two Generations—A Study of Black Urban Families and Their Children." Journal of Child Psychology and Psychiatry 16: 125-40.

Rotter, J. 1966. "Generalized Expectancies for Internal Versus External Control of Reinforcement." Psychological Monographs 80(1): 1-28.

Scrimshaw, N. S. 1968. "Early Malnutrition and Central Nervous System Function." Merrill-Palmer Quarterly 15: 375-88.

Seldin, N. E. 1972. "The Family of the Addict: A Review of the Literature." International Journal of the Addictions 7: 97-107.

Sowder, B. J. 1977. "Children of Addicts and Other Problem Families: A Review of Literature." Xeroxed. Bethesda, Md.: Burt Associates.

____. 1973. "The Poor in the Affluent Society." In Social Change and the Mental Health of Children, edited by the Joint Commission on Mental Health of Children, pp. 17-88. New York: Harper and Row.

____. 1972. "Socialization Determinants in the Development and Modification of Intergroup and Intragroup Behaviors." In Research Problems and Issues in the Area of Socialization, edited by B. J. Sowder and J. B. Lazar, pp. 1-228. Washington, D.C.: Social Research Group.

Sowder, B. J., and E. D. Wish. 1979. "The Use of Family Counseling in Selected Drug Abuse Treatment Agencies." Xeroxed. Bethesda, Md.: Burt Associates.

Strauss, M. E., R. H. Starr, E. M. Ostrea, C. J. Chavez, and J. C. Stryker. 1976. "Behavioral Concomitants of Prenatal Addiction to Narcotics." Journal of Pediatrics 89: 842-46.

Sullivan, N. D., and R. P. Fleshman. 1975-76. "Paternal Deprivation in Male Heroin Addicts." Drug Forum 5: 75-80.

Taylor, S. D., M. Wilbur, and R. Osnos. 1966. "The Wives of Drug Addicts." American Journal of Psychiatry 123: 585-91.

Tennant, F., R. Detels, and V. Clark. 1975. "Some Childhood Antecedents of Drug and Alcohol Abuse." American Journal of Epidemiology 102: 377-85.

Terman, L., and M. A. Merrill. 1973. Stanford-Binet Intelligence Scale, 1972 Norm Edition. Boston: Houghton Mifflin.

U.S., Department of Health, Education, and Welfare. 1975. Health Attitudes and Behavior of Youths 12-17 Years: Demographic and Socioeconomic Factors, United States. Washington, D.C.: Government Printing Office.

U.S., Department of Health, Education, and Welfare. National Center for Health Statistics. 1969. Vital and Health Statistics Programs and Collection Procedures. Plan of Operation of a Health Examination of U.S. Youths 12-17 Years of Age. Washington, D.C.: Government Printing Office.

U.S., Public Health Service. 1976. Teenage Smoking—National Patterns of Cigarette Smoking, Ages 12 through 18, in 1972 and 1974. Washington, D.C.: Government Printing Office.

Vaillant, G. E. 1970. "The Natural History of Narcotic Drug Addiction." Seminars in Psychiatry 2: 486-98.

____. 1966. "A Twelve-year Follow-up of New York Narcotic Addicts: IV. Some Characteristics and Determinants of Abstinence." American Journal of Psychiatry 123: 573-85.

Webb, K. W., M. R. Burt, F. G. Friedman, L. Kanin, I. Kundra, B. Sowder, and L. Webb. 1975. "Report and Plan on Recommended Approaches and Methods for Determination of National Incidence of Child Abuse and Neglect, Vol. I." Xeroxed. Bethesda, Md.: Burt Associates.

Wilson, G. S., M. M. Desmond, and W. M. Verniaud. 1973. "Early Development of Infants of Heroin-addicted Mothers." American Journal of Diseases of Children 126: 457-62.

Wilson, G. S., R. McCready, J. Kean, and J. Baxter. 1979. "The Development of Preschool Children of Heroin-addicted Mothers: A Controlled Study." Pediatrics 63: 135-41.

Wolk, R. L., and M. H. Diskind. 1961. "Personality Dynamics of Mothers and Wives of Drug Addicts." Crime and Delinquency 7: 148-52.

INDEX

ABOUT THE AUTHORS

BARBARA J. SOWDER is senior vice-president of Burt Associates Incorporated and its affiliate organization, the Institute for Human Resources Research at Bethesda, Maryland. Until 1975, she was a psychologist at the National Institute of Mental Health, a staff member of various research companies, and research director of the Joint Commission on Mental Health of Children.

Sowder has prepared numerous reports for federal agencies on children and families and the systems that provide them services. Several have been published and widely circulated by federal agencies. She collaborated in several books published by the Joint Commission on Mental Health of Children.

Sowder holds a B.A., M.A., and Ph.D. from George Washington University, Washington, D.C.

MARVIN R. BURT has been president of Burt Associates Incorporated and the Institute for Human Resources Research at Bethesda, Maryland, since 1972. He was previously a member of the senior research staff of a large, nonprofit research organization. He has published six books and 22 research monographs (many published by government agencies). Most of his publications deal with children at risk and drug abuse.

Burt holds a B.A. degree from U.C.L.A. and M.P.A. and D.P.A. degrees from George Washington University.